WEST
SUPER-MARE
A History and Guide

WESTON
SUPER-MARE
A History and Guide

PHILIP
BEISLY

ALAN SUTTON
1988

Alan Sutton Publishing Limited
Brunswick Road · Gloucester

First published 1988

British Library Cataloguing in Publication Data

Beisly, Philip
Weston-super-Mare : a history and guide.
1.   Avon. Weston-super-Mare, to 1987
I.   Title
942.3′96

ISBN 0-86299-509-4

Published in association with the Weston-super-Mare Heritage
Centre, Weston-super-Mare Civic Society, 3–6 Wadham Street,
Weston-super-Mare.

Cover illustration: the Esplanade in the 1840s, looking north
towards Knightstone, from a print published by Joseph Whereat.

Typesetting and origination by
Alan Sutton Publishing Limited
Printed in Great Britain

Contents

Preface and Acknowledgements

This book traces the story of Weston-super-Mare with special reference to the sites, buildings and monuments that can be seen today. The principal interest lies in the growth and character of the Victorian resort, for Britain invented the seaside and Weston-super-Mare is a classic example of the British watering place. However this part of the story is only the centrepiece, and the book traces the settlement's older history and its more recent past.

A number of Factsheets are published by Woodspring Museum in Burlington Street, and Weston Civic Society has produced a series of Trails, available at the Heritage Centre in Wadham Street. These leaflets will guide and assist those interested in further exploration.

I am grateful to those who have read and commented on the text: Mary Harding, Robert Smart, and Martin Taylor. Nicholas Corcos gave me guidance on Weston's early history, and Dr Peter Miller supplied useful information on the local quarrying industry. I have also profited from numerous conversations with Brian Austin, covering many aspects of the town's story. I received kind assistance from Woodspring Museum, the *Weston Mercury*, Mr Chris Crook of the Landmark Trust, Councillor Elfan ap Rees, and the Somerset County Records Office, and also from Mr John Bailey, Mr Clive Jackson and Mr Michael Woods of Woodspring District Council. I owe a large debt of gratitude to Mr John Loosley of Woodspring Central Library; the Library's Local History Room contains a rich store of guidebooks, maps, newspapers and periodicals, local government records, and the local census returns.

The bulk of the older photographs are reproduced by kind permission of Woodspring Central Library. For modern photographs and original maps and drawings I thank the staff of the Civic Society's Heritage Project, and especially Raymond Dwerryhouse, from whose advice and comments I derived much benefit. For permission to reproduce other photographs I am grateful to Dr. Howard Smith, Mr Andrew Eddy, Woodspring Museum, the *Weston Mercury*, and the British Rotorcraft Museum.

I am conscious of a more general debt of gratitude to all those with whom, at various times, I have discussed the story of Weston-super-Mare: I have probably stored up many facts and ideas from these conversations which I am now producing as my own without acknowledgement. Any omissions of this kind are unintentional, and any errors are my own.

Early History

Most modern visitors to Weston-super-Mare approach the town across the great plain of the Northmarsh, the northern section of the Somerset Levels, and see, rising before them like an island, the mass of Worlebury Hill. It was indeed an island at times in the prehistoric past, when sea levels were higher and the waters of the Severn Estuary reached many miles farther inland than they do today. Even when the modern coastline had become stabilised and sand dunes had formed to consolidate it, much of the Northmarsh was a swampy terrain drained by sluggish streams and rivers. It was only when the village of Weston was already turning into a resort, in the early years of the nineteenth century, that centuries of piecemeal draining of this landscape was brought to completion. The village discovered by earlier visitors was still an isolated settlement clinging to the hillside.

Worlebury Hill largely consists of carboniferous limestone, an outcrop of the rock forming the main mass of the Mendip Hills. Limestone country has an ancient feeling; its clean line brings one close to the rock beneath, which outcrops constantly and lies about the surface. The historian Collinson described Worlebury thus in 1791:

> This mountain is an immense rock of limestone, with but very little herbage intermixed; yet here and there a solitary sheep is seen pasturing on its naked, barren ridge, which, being elevated far above the surrounding country, and overlooking the long tract of the Severn Sea, is buffeted by every blast.

The highest point, in fact, is only 356 feet above sea level, but the contrast between the upland scenery of Mendip and the surrounding levels makes the hills seem higher than they are. The planting of Weston Woods and the spread of building have altered our perceptions of Worlebury. To early visitors the village looked much like dozens of others in the Mendip region: near the bottom of the hill was a small church and its Glebe

In common with most Mendip villages, the settlements in the Weston area were close to the sides of the hills. The low-lying moors between the hills were liable to flooding.

House; Grove Cottage next door, the seat of the Lord of the Manor; and a huddle of farms and cottages facing the open wastes of the Northmarsh behind the sand dunes. Fields stretched along the hillside, and the skyline was dominated by the ruins of the Celtic or 'Ancient British' fort which had been the home of 'the old men' long ago.

The area was occupied in the New Stone Age and the Bronze Age, and burials and implements from these times have been found on the hill. The Celts, builders of the hill fort, left no written record of themselves, unlike some of the contemporary races in Europe in the centuries immediately before the birth of Christ. They remain in prehistory, and their culture must be reconstructed from archaeological evidence. Worlebury fort was

2

a source of great interest to many of Weston's nineteenth century visitors, who were often keen antiquarians. Some of them helped to lay the foundations of modern archaeology in this area, and the excavation of the fort by the Reverend Francis Warre in 1851 is considered to have been the first proper archaeological excavation of its type. Techniques of excavation and the interpretation of finds have made enormous strides since then, and many of the myths concerning the ancient Britons have since been dispelled.

The hill fort is one of a chain of defensive sites in Mendip Country, of a type that reached full development in the late Iron Age, in the century or two before the birth of Christ. These forts are evidence of a well organised and populous society. Even today, when the site is covered by trees and the walls of the fort are heaps of stone, a walk around the site brings home to one the scale of the construction and the engineering achievement involved in the work. Worlebury fort encloses more than ten acres and is the second biggest Iron Age site on the Mendips: only Dolebury (eighteen acres) is larger.

A plan of the Worlebury Hillfort, based on Dymond. The fort is at the seaward end of Worlebury Hill above Weston, and is now hidden from the town below by Weston Woods. On its northern side are cliffs which complete the defensive ring made by the massive walls and ditches.

The walls were originally proper masonry constructions with rubble infilling. Watch-towers flanked the great wooden gates of the three entrances, while the eastern approaches, on the level hilltop, had deep outer ditches and additional ramparts to deter the enemy. The defenders used the slingshot, and the design of the defences anticipates engagement with attackers at a distance. Stores of pebbles gathered from the beach below have been found inside the fort. Such a massively defended site would have been of little value in the earlier days of hand-to-hand fighting.

With its secure position and extensive views, the advantages of such a site for the tribe in the warlike times of the later Iron Age are evident. However the fully developed fort, probably built between the third and the first centuries BC, was an extension of an earlier site which occupied the western tip of the hilltop. If this earlier site was fortified at all its defences were more elementary. It is probably wrong to see even the later fort in purely military terms. Worlebury (which later gave its name to the whole hill) may also have been something of a status symbol for the tribe, acting as the centre of local government, commerce, religion and tribal life. Such forts have been compared to the walled towns and cities of medieval times. Most of the population of the area lived outside the walls, farming from small scattered sites, grazing animals and cultivating the small fields which could still be traced on the hill 150 years ago. The fort itself has an outer enclosure for animals, to the east of the main ramparts and ditches. Although the Celtic peasants could withdraw to the fort in time of danger, they probably spent most of their lives in the outlying settlements, some of which may have been the precursors of the villages we know today. Celtic pit burials have been found in Grove Park and Stafford Place. The Celts undoubtedly exploited the marshy lands surrounding Worlebury for fishing and hunting.

Inside the fort there are numerous pits cut into the rock. At one time these were held to have been the dwellings of the 'savage' inmates, but we now know them to have been dug by the relatively sophisticated occupants of the site as storage pits for grain. The tops of the pits were sealed with clay and considerable quantities of grain could have been kept in these Iron Age stores, giving a supply of food during winter months or in the event of crop failure or seige. It has been suggested that grain may even have been exported from Worlebury, since such a trade

Inside the fort two thousand years ago. Some of the hut sites have been revealed by recent clearance.

is thought to have flourished in late Iron Age Britain when yields were probably very high. Older storage pits at Worlebury were later used by the inhabitants as rubbish dumps.

The dwellings of the fort's Celtic occupants would actually have been round huts, made of wooden uprights and wickerwork covered with mud or clay. They probably had thatched roofs and a central hearth from which the smoke escaped through a hole in the apex of the roof. Circular remains were noted by early nineteenth century visitors, and recorded on plans, but all traces were lost as the trees grew to maturity and undergrowth became established. However recent clearance work organised by Woodspring Museum and supervised by Mr Chris Richards, has enabled the sites of at least three hut circles to be identified again after a century and a half, and indeed a number of other possible circles, not shown on earlier plans, have also been found.

North Somerset and South Gloucestershire was the territory of the Dobunni tribe in the later Iron Age. The Celts of this time were increasingly involved in trade with the continent, and therefore had a degree of contact with the Roman Empire for some time before the Roman invasion of Britain in the first century AD. Even discounting such influences, it is evident from finds of jewellery and pottery that the Celtic culture was one in which taste had achieved high standards, and ornament and refinement were prized in everyday life. Whatever the Romans might have thought, Celtic society had become genuinely civilised in many ways, and the natives of this country were far from being the uncouth savages they were once thought to be.

The Roman invasion came in AD 43, and it is thought that the conquest of this part of Britain was complete six years later. The discovery within Worlebury fort of several skulls, one with seven sword cuts, once prompted speculation that the site was taken by the invaders in bloody battle, but it is equally likely that the grisly remains date from a time of inter-tribal warfare among the native population. The Roman presence was quickly established and consolidated in North Somerset after the invasion. The lead mines at Charterhouse, originally run by the military, were a major industrial site, and much of the lead was exported to the continent. Charterhouse lead has been identified at Pompeii. In addition it was probably used at Bath, and in the numerous villas (or Romanised farms) which began to dot the landscape. The nearest villa site to Worlebury of which we are currently aware is at Locking, close to the present RAF camp; the villa here was quite a large one. There was a Romano-British temple on Brean Down, across the Axe mouth, built in the middle of the fourth century. It has often been maintained that the port of Uphill, at the southern end of Weston Bay by the Axe, was used to export Mendip lead, and that a Roman road led along the hills to Uphill from Charterhouse, but we cannot be certain of this. Most roads are very ancient and date at least from Celtic times, and simply continued in use during the Roman occupation; but there is no evidence of a Roman road to Uphill in the sense in which this is normally understood. The existence of other routes for the movement of lead from Charterhouse has been demonstrated rather more surely, but no doubt Uphill, sited as it was at the mouth of an important waterway and offering safe anchorage by high ground, saw much trade during Roman times and in succeeding ages.

In the Weston area the evidence from this period is scanty, but there is sufficient to demonstrate continuing occupation. Roman pottery was found when the foundations of the Technical College were being excavated in the 1960s, together with coins

The Uphill Pill joins the Axe Estuary and was a safe harbour by the mouth of one of the county's major waterways. The cliffs in the background are the result of nineteenth and early twentieth century quarrying.

and beads, and there have been other finds in this vicinity between Lower Church Road, Knightstone, and Royal Crescent. One may suppose that the native population continued to occupy the old settlements and farm the same fields on Worlebury Hill under Roman rule, even though the fort itself was abandoned.

The Roman occupation seems to have collapsed finally in the early years of the fifth century. There is no evidence that the fort of Worlebury was reoccupied by the native population, although this is known to have happened elsewhere, notably at South Cadbury, where the Celtic leader whom we know as King Arthur is believed to have had his headquarters. Nevertheless the period between about 400 and 700 AD almost certainly saw a reversion to Celtic ways as Roman influence faded. In the sixth and seventh centuries Celtic Christian missionaries are thought to have been active along the coastal region of the county. Tradition has it that St. Congar founded a monastery at Congresbury.

Perhaps there was a St. Kew at Kewstoke. The church of St. Bridget at Brean has been held to have a Celtic dedication. And of course, throughout the Dark Ages the ancient Christian centre of Glastonbury was a beacon of religious life and learning. It is not too fanciful to see the River Axe as an important route for traffic and communication in this regard, for the River Brue, which skirts Glastonbury, is believed to have fed into the Axe near Bleadney until the monks had it diverted later in the medieval period. So the Axe may well have been a more significant waterway in former times, and thus a major 'highway'.

The Saxons did not occupy Somerset until well into the seventh century, the Battle of Peonnan in 658 being the crucial breakthrough. With them we enter a time of greater documentation and feel ourselves in a more familiar landscape, not least because so many of our place names are of Saxon origin. Weston itself is one such – it is the west tun (tun = place, farmstead, or estate). But a Saxon place name does not prove that a settlement was founded in Saxon times. Saxon names often replaced the older Celtic names of long established settlements, as the native Celtic population was gradually absorbed into Saxon society.

With Weston one is bound to ask the question: west of what? Other directional names around Worlebury Hill – such as Norton, the north tun, and Milton, the middle tun – seem to imply the existence of a central predominant settlement. Nicholas Corcos has suggested that Worle is the most obvious candidate. It was certainly the most important of the Worlebury villages in later times; the Domesday Book of 1086 shows it as by far the richest. Perhaps we see here traces of an older system under which the whole of the Worlebury area was originally one unit, including the tuns or dispersed farmsteads that gradually developed into more independent settlements.

By the time of the Domesday Book, twenty years after the Norman Conquest, this process may have been well advanced, although Weston is not named as a separate manor. It is thought to have formed part of the manor of 'Aisecombe' or Ashcombe, which survived as a small hamlet to the east of Weston until nineteenth century development spread out towards it. Throughout Victorian times Ashcombe Manor Farm remained on the hillside where Manor Road is today.

The Domesday Book records other manors whose names we can still recognise: Opopille or Uphill at the south end of the bay; Chiwestock or Kewstoke; Mideltone or Milton, which remained linked to Kewstoke, although on the other side of the hill; and Worle, where a small 'motte and bailey' fort at Castle Batch was built in Norman times. There was also the manor of Worspring, or Woodspring, at Middle Hope to the north of Sand Bay, and it may be that there was a settlement here which disappeared after the foundation of Woodspring Priory at the beginning of the thirteenth century. The Priory ruins still stand, the last monastic ruins of Mendip, and the site is now owned by the Landmark Trust. This was a small house of Augustinian Canons, of the Order of St. Victor, which later acquired the manors of Worle and Locking. These manors were all in the Hundred of Winterstoke. The exact location of Winterstoke is unknown, but it is thought to have been in the Banwell area. At some point Weston and Ashcombe became separate manors and records dating from the reign of Henry III show that the two manors were both held by the Arthur family of Clapton, near Portishead.

It is only in the centuries following the Domesday Survey that we find clear evidence of the existence of Weston as a village. Documents of 1226 refer to the church of St. John at Weston,

Woodspring Priory, drawn by John Rutter 1829.

9

which was to pay 100 pounds of wax annually to the Cathedral at Wells. And it is in medieval church records that we first find the version of the name which has endured, Weston-super-Mare. This is not a Victorian invention, as is sometimes thought, but the coinage of a medieval cleric writing on the eve of the Black Death in 1348, seeking, we imagine, to distinguish the village from the many other Westons in Somerset. 'Super Mare' is simply Latin for 'on, or above, the sea'. The Registers of the Dean and Chapter of Wells reveal other *ad hoc* ways of identifying the village which failed to catch on: 'Weston-propre-Worle' in 1233, 'Weston-juxta-Worle' in 1311, 'Weston-juxta-Mare', 'Weston-upon-More'. The Norman church appears to have been modified, but not substantially rebuilt, judging by drawings which show it before the rebuilding of 1824. During this rebuilding, Norman

A thirteenth-century dripstone terminal excavated at Woodspring Priory. *Andrew Eddy.*

details were discovered – a simple round-headed window and some gargoyles – and they can be examined in Woodspring Museum.

So how old is Weston? While documentary evidence takes us back only to the early thirteenth century, it is impossible not to believe that the thread of continuity stretches back much farther. The document of 1226 concerns an existing church. Most Norman churches were rebuildings of Saxon wooden churches, and very few were entirely new foundations. We note that St. John's was a parish church by 1226, indicating the existence of an established community, (although there never seems to have been a church at Ashcombe, which had perhaps been more significant and had given its name to the manor at some time before the Domesday Survey). Weston almost certainly existed as a distinct settlement, and perhaps even as a parish, before the Norman Conquest.

To the east of Grove Park, which we know was the home of the Lord of the Manor in later times, lay The Worthy, shown on early nineteenth century maps; the name survives in Worthy Lane (now Market Lane) and Worthy Place. 'Worthy' or 'worth' is one

Weston Old Church.

The church of St. John the Baptist, Weston-super-Mare, demolished in 1824, was typical of churches in the poorer villages of the district. It received some modifications in the later middle ages but was never substantially enlarged. *Rutter.*

11

The shaft of the medieval churchyard cross outside the south wall of the present church. A carving set in one of the walls inside the tower may well be the missing head.

of the most common Saxon place names and means basically 'enclosure'. It often indicates the approximate site of an Anglo-Saxon farmstead. Another such element found in field names is 'hay' or 'hays' (fence, enclosure), which we find in Blakehay, the name of the field between High Street and Wadham Street immediately to the south of Grove Park ('blake' = black, usually explained in this context as referring to areas of particularly dark soil arising from long periods of human habitation or cultivation). The proximity of the manorial house and the church pinpoint this neighbourhood as the focus of Saxon settlement.

It is surely no coincidence that the cluster of Romano-British finds lies only yards from St. John's church and Grove Park. Continuity in the occupation of sites during the Celtic, Romano-British and Saxon periods is now stressed by historians and archaeologists, for while military and political upheavals may have changed the rulers and the ruling aristocracy, farming and the day-to-day lives of the ordinary people carried on much as before. For it is primarily the logic of the landscape itself which determines human occupation and exploitation, and this logic did not significantly change over the centuries. The deeper soil of the hillside remained the best place to grow crops; the sheltered 'coombes' such as Grove Park remained the ideal sites for farmsteads; and the water supply remained where the springs gushed out of the limestone hill near its base. When we trace the village seen by the first visitors we are also tracing the outlines of a centuries-old pattern of settlement. The early nineteenth century maps of the village, drawn when resort development was just gathering pace, show us something of this ancient logic of the landscape.

The village appears to have had two open fields since medieval times, the East Field and the West Field. The former lay beyond The Worthy and above the Bristol Road. The latter covered the area we know as The Shrubbery and beyond. Early nineteenth century maps show the remains of these medieval common fields clearly, although by that time they had been reduced by various piecemeal divisions and enclosures. The largest of these is shown as the West Tining or Tyning (the word actually means 'enclosure'). As with other villages along the side of Mendip, we can see how the fields pushed up the slope to a point where the soil became too shallow to be useful. The open hilltop above was used for grazing animals. This ancient boundary between the fields and the open hilltop was preserved by the

West Tyning

West Field

Tor Field

East Field

Knightstone

1. The Grove
2. Parish Church
3. Leeves Cottage
4. Well Close

The village of Weston-super-Mare before enclosure, at the beginning of the nineteenth century. The outline of the open fields can still be traced.

Parliamentary enclosure settlement of 1815 and is the line we know today as South Road and Cecil Road.

The majority of the buildings in the village as it is recorded were set back from the shore and straggled down 'The Street' and onto the moor. The Street is our High Street, while Watersill Road is our Regent Street and Locking Road. At the south end of the Street was what looks like an earlier enclosure from the moor, called 'Wallclose', presumably the origin of our Walliscote Road. Meadow Lane is obviously the start of our Meadow Street, although it only went as far as our Orchard Place. West Lane is our West Street. Dark Lane or Grove Lane wound up the hill beside Grove Park to become what is now Queen's Road. The development of what we conjecture to have been the Saxon settlement in the direction of the moor may reflect a reluctance to occupy good arable land on the hillside, and perhaps indicates a

14

A reconstruction by Raymond Dwerryhouse of the view from the village street, looking north from the site of the Italian Gardens in High Street.

degree of 'drying out' or better management of the wet flat land over the centuries. Along much of the coastal Levels there is a strip of ground fronting the sea which is slightly higher than the ground farther inland. It is the result of clay deposits from the estuary and drifting sand. This strip is quite narrow at Weston, but it can be traced today in changes of level in the High Street area: village Weston took advantage of the slightly higher ground.

A small stream ran down the hillside from a spring where Coombe Road is now. On reaching The Street near its north end and Grove Park, the stream turned south to run along the east side of the Street, before turning east to run inland and join the system of man-made drainage ditches or rhynes (pronounced 'reens') that all eventually drain to the Uphill Pill and the River Axe. However, one is bound to speculate that this stream may have originally pursued a more direct route to the sea along West Lane. Local lore still speaks of an old watercourse under the Technical College, and the state of the cellars at the Heritage Centre in Wadham Street appears to support such a notion. So does the fact that two paths ran from the beach, as if either side of the stream's former course. Whether the old course became blocked naturally or deliberately is an interesting speculation.

The village was at the north end of the bay, and this is the point where high tides threaten the land most, as the modern visitor standing opposite the Winter Gardens Pavilion can often

15

observe. The area of the church and Grove Park is above flood level, but most of the village was often in danger. Sea walls were maintained by the parishioners, probably since medieval times; obligations to maintain sections of the walls were among the duties involved in local forms of land tenure. From time to time, however, the sea breached the defences, usually when high tides were driven by a strong west wind.

The commoners' rights naturally included the grazing of animals on both the hilltop and the moor, although the land belonged to the Lord of the Manor. At certain times of the year the steward of the manor had all the beasts and horses driven off the moor to one spot, at the same time assembling their owners. Those who had pasture rights would swear an oath claiming the right, while trespassers were fined. Thus a document of July 1801, recording this ancient custom and entitled 'The usual Rules for driving Weston Moor', says:

> To go to the mark on Uphill Green towards Mrs Kniftings for every person to swear to his stock if required, and for every poor person of the parish of Weston to pay 10s. if not a common, and all other trespassers at the option of Mr. Pigott or the Parishioners the whole of the stock to be driven on Ashcombe Batch, and the money left after all expenses is paid to be laid out in necessary articles in the parish.

Such manorial customs, adapted to local circumstances, obtained in most villages before parliamentary enclosure, and were survivals from medieval times. They enshrined the balance of rights and duties between the lord of the manor and the villagers. Commoners claimed their rights through holding an 'auster' tenement: the word 'auster', commonly used in Somerset, is derived from the Latin 'austrum' (a tenement held in villeinage of the Lord), but was often thought to mean 'ancient'. The word itself was sometimes corrupted, and Westonians used to boast that they held an 'oyster' tenement.

At Weston the rights of the austers covered fishing as well as farming, for this was an important part of the local economy. The Severn Estuary offered better fishing than it does today. Salmon were regularly caught, and local tradition required the first salmon of the season to be offered to the Lord of the Manor. Sprats were landed in large quantities. Most local fishing was done with nets, not from boats. The nets were stretched between stakes

The ancient fishery at Birnbeck Island before the pier was built. The line of nets between the stakes on the right follows the shingle causeway which is uncovered at low tide.

driven into the bed at low tide. Fishing rights concerned the use of the stakes or 'stalls' at the traditional fisheries at Anchor Head and Birnbeck (where stakes can still be seen along the natural shingle causeway that connects the island with the mainland). The fish were caught in the submerged nets at high tide, when the currents ran strongly along the headland, and were held as the tide ebbed. Unfortunately the gulls often got to the exposed catch before the fishermen, so 'gull yellers' were employed to bellow at the birds to frighten them off. One famous gull yeller is said to have been audible as far inland as Congresbury with a following wind.

Fish were an important source of protein in medieval times and later, especially in days when meat was more of a luxury than it is now. Much of the catch was taken to market inland. Fishing rights were therefore valuable, and jealously guarded, as we see from the incomplete record of a dispute of 1492 between John Payne and the Arthur family of Clapton Court, Lords of the Manor of Weston at that time. Payne accused John Arthur of forcibly and illegally fishing in his fishery at Anchor Head and stated that Arthur's men 'by force of arms namely with sticks and knives fished in the several (i.e. private) fishery . . . and took and carried away thence fish namely 100 horse loads of fish called Barons 400 fish called Tubbelyns 300 haddockes and 200 whit-ynges and inflicted other enormities'. He claimed that he had sustained damage to the amount of £26, a large sum in those days. We do not know how the case ended.

Fishing rights were enjoyed by villagers from Worle and Kewstoke, many of whom walked to and from the fisheries every day. The path along the top of Worlebury Hill, which emerges opposite Birnbeck Causeway, is known as the Fishermens' Path. At one point along its length, about 200 yards west of the reservoir, is Picwinner Cairn, a heap of stones on which local fishermen on their way to the shore would throw a stone for luck, repeating this couplet:

> Picwinner, Picwinner,
> Give me a good dinner.

This is probably an ancient site. The old lane from Weston, passing the site of the Town Quarry, joined the top path here. Perhaps the cairn was originally an ancient tumulus, or a Saxon boundary mark.

Not many villagers could afford boats. The boat-building trade in this area seems to have been carried on partly for the benefit of leading farmers during later centuries; there was a considerable trade in importing sheep and cattle from Wales. The wealthier fishermen who did use boats sailed in Weston 'flatners', shallow-bottomed craft which were suited to fishing in the bay. Knightstone Island was the local anchorage; like Birnbeck it was reached by a pebble causeway, over which boats could sail at high tide.

The local fishermen had another trade in the eighteenth and early nineteenth centuries. Smuggling flourished along these quiet shores during years when the import duties on luxury goods were high. Brandy, tobacco, lace and other goods were run ashore at night and hidden until they could be safely moved away, perhaps to be sold to the local squirearchy or to the aristocrats and rich merchants of Bristol or Bath. The sand dunes or 'tots' at the end of Watersill Road (Regent Street) were said to have been a favourite hiding place for contraband cargo. The excisemen patrolled the coast, usually in vain, for the villagers signalled with lights to waiting boats in the Channel to indicate safe landing places. However there were sometimes dramatic pursuits and hair's-breadth escapes; two local fishermen at

Weston fishermen of the nineteenth century.

Uphill escaped capture by running away through half a dozen local parishes during one night, and then had to do a normal day's work to avoid suspicion. When they returned to the scene of the crime they found that their boat had been sawn in half as a punishment. The area of Prince Consort Gardens, above Birnbeck, was formerly called Flagstaff Hill after the flagstaff used by the coastguards to signal to the revenue cutter when dirty work was suspected, so that there were two rival systems of communication at work simultaneously. Early Victorian visitors to the resort could still benefit from the thrills, and the rewards, of local smuggling. In 1845 the *Weston Gazette* reported that 240 barrels of contraband spirits had been landed at St. Thomas's Head near Woodspring Priory, and in 1846 there was a sale of contraband and condemned merchandise at the Victoria Concert Room. Smuggling declined after the 1840s, once Free Trade Reforms had lifted many of the import duties on luxury goods.

Early nineteenth century visitors could also see another local industry still in operation, mining on the Worlebury hillside. The east end of the hill achieved national importance as a source

The old church of St. Nicholas on the hill at Uphill, now partly ruined, contains Norman work. It was a navigation point for sailors. St. Nicholas is the patron saint of mariners. *Andrew Eddy.*

of calamine, a zinc ore, in the sixteenth century. It was thought that the ore was discovered in 1566 by German prospectors on land belonging to Sir Henry Wallop, but Nicholas Corcos has discovered evidence that mining was taking place on the hill much earlier in the century, possibly under the aegis of Woodspring Priory. In Elizabethan times, however, the mining rights were leased to the new Society of Mineral and Battery Works, which 'set Tenne or Twelve persons straungers and Englishe on worke to moyne and search for Calamine, which the Countrymen ther do reporte, and gott 20: or 30: tonnes of the said stone'. The ore was found in veins up to three feet thick and the 'gruffy ground' created by lead and calamine mining still covers areas of the hill, chiefly above Milton and near the fort. Calamine was required to blend with copper in order to produce brass, an alloy increasingly in demand in sixteenth century England for both military and industrial purposes. The Society of Mineral and

Battery Works was granted rights to mine calamine and manufacture brass and brass wire by new methods in 1565, these skills
having been learnt in Germany, which was then the acknow-
ledged centre of European metal working.

The company thought of establishing a brass foundry at
Bristol, but eventually began work at Tintern on the River Wye,
where calamine from Worlebury Hill was taken by boat. The
production of brass seems to have been still experimental and
did not proceed well. In 1582 the company leased its rights to
four partners who opened a new brass mill in Middlesex: 'the
oar, or earth ... is brought out of Somersetshire from Mendip
hills, the most from 'Worley hill'. Other Mendip mines were
developed. Broadfield Down above Wrington was a major source
in the seventeenth century and deposits on the main Mendip
range began to be worked at the same time. But the Worlebury
mines seem to have been worked into the nineteenth century, at
least intermittently, and John Rutter speaks of them as if they
were still in operation in 1829. In addition, lead was mined near
Christchurch until 1845, and yellow ochre in the Hazeldene
Road area until the 1920s.

WHAT TO SEE

● Geology: limestone stratification at Uphill Quarry and Town
Quarry.

● Worlebury Hill fort in Weston Woods.

● Finds from Worlebury in Woodspring Museum.

● Street pattern and layout in Grove Park area.

● Old church of St. Nicholas, Uphill (on the hill).

● St. John's, Lower Church Road: remains of cross outside south
wall, and carving set in the wall inside the tower.

● Woodspring Priory (approach from North Worle).

● Birnbeck Fishery: shingle causeway to island and stakes
(visible at low tide).

The Young Resort

Seaside resorts developed during the eighteenth century, eventually displacing the inland spas in fashion and favour. Scarborough had become the first watering place almost by accident, because the mineral springs which made it a spa happened to be by the shore. In 1751 Dr Richard Russell published an influential medical treatise on the benefits of the seaside cure and opened a bathing infirmary at Brighton. Later in the century the Prince Regent adopted Brighton and King George III patronised Weymouth. Many resorts grew up in the second half of the century. They offered an alternative to the polite and formalised world of the inland spas at a time when taste was changing in favour of relaxation and simplicity. There was a growing interest in landscape and scenery, heightened at the turn of the century by the Romantic movement in literature.

Most resorts were regional in their appeal, and, as Dr Bryan Brown has pointed out, Bristol and Bath, with their large concentration of the rich and leisured classes, formed the biggest potential body of seaside visitors outside London. However, Bristol was a conservative city and seems to have been late in adopting the seaside habit. Difficulties in travelling weighed against Bristol and Bath establishing a significant connection with South Coast resorts such as Weymouth or Lyme Regis, although attempts were made to develop such a link, and the way remained open for the upper classes from England's second city and from the Queen of the Spas to discover the local coastline of the Severn Estuary.

Weston appears to have come to the notice of outside visitors first through the network of the North Somerset squirearchy. The manor of Weston had belonged to the Pigott family since 1696. The Pigotts owned numerous manors between Weston and Bristol, and the main seat was at Brockley. They intermarried with the Smyths of Ashton Court, becoming the Smyth-Pigotts in the early nineteenth century. They were an influential family

Grove House at the beginning of the nineteenth century, after the first of the Pigotts' improvements. The steps and some of the walls survive. The house may have incorporated much older work, and perhaps marked the spot of the original farmstead from which Weston grew.

THE GROVE, WESTON SUPER MARE.

Grove House after its enlargement by John Hugh Smyth Pigott in the 1830s.

whose portraits were painted by Gainsborough in Bath. The family appears to have taken a fresh interest in its Weston property during the time of John Pigott (1741–1816), and his second brother, the Reverend Wadham Pigott, was curate-in-charge of the parish by 1790. Wadham was resident in the village and became in effect acting squire, perhaps because of his brother's absences abroad.

During the 1770s or 1780s Grove Cottage or Grove House was modernised, and in 1783, the neighbouring Glebe House was similarly improved. No doubt Wadham Pigott entertained guests at Weston, and before long the Glebe House was being let to staying visitors. The village appealed to members of a social group alert to new fashions and tastes who were wealthy enough to follow their inclinations. One of the first recorded visitors was Hannah More, the well known writer, philanthropist, and educational reformer, who had made her home at Barley Wood, Wrington. She stayed at Uphill (it is thought at Rose Cottage) for health reasons in 1773, and while here formed the acquaintance of Dr John Langhorne, classical scholar and Rector of Blagdon, who was staying at Weston. In an article in *The Gentleman's Magazine* in 1805 George Bennett, a solicitor from Rolstone near Banwell and a keen antiquarian, wrote:

> This village is much frequented of late in Summer and Autumn for the benefit of sea air and bathing; several good lodging-houses having been lately erected for the reception of company. And the Revd. Mr Leeves of Wrington has built a charming little cottage on the beach, at which himself and family reside a considerable part of the year.

This confirms that Weston was being frequented some years earlier than has generally been thought, although the number of visitors was probably tiny. It is interesting to learn of lodging houses being purpose-built in the very first years of the century, presumably indicating that visitors had already been arriving in sufficient numbers and over a long enough period to lead the unknown builders to have confidence that the phenomenon was not a flash in the pan. Leeves' Cottage 'on the beach' is said to have been built in 1791, a year or two at least after the clergyman's first visit. Part of the building, the Old Thatched Cottage, still stands at the corner of Knightstone Road, and is now the only thatched building in Weston. Its size and character indicate how much the fashionable taste was for going 'back to nature' in something not too different from the farms and cottages of the villagers. It may have been only a 'pretend' cottage, but how different from the elegant town houses of Georgian Bath!

One is bound to conjecture that both Dr Langhorne and the Revd Leeves were in Weston in part because of the presence of the Revd Wadham Pigott, who, besides being an 'elegant and popular preacher', was also a friendly and amenable companion. His presence in the coastal village certainly explains the visits of the artist George Cumberland between 1802 and 1806. Cumberland was a friend of his, and stayed at the Glebe House, spending much of his time sketching in the parish. He was a friend of William Blake, and became an influential figure in the Bristol School of artists.

The beauty and interest of the scenery was a vital part of the appeal of the village to these early visitors. Although the sea itself was rather muddy, this was a delightful and romantic spot, with its wide shallow beach and curving bay, the headland of Brean Down and the islands of Steep Holm and Flat Holm in the

Leeves' Cottage, built 'on the beach' at the end of the eighteenth century. The right hand section can still be seen.

middle distance, and Exmoor and the Welsh coast visible farther off. Worlebury Hill protected the village nestling on its southern slope. It is again the logic of the landscape, rather than some undiscovered historical evidence, which explains the birth of the resort in the last thirty years of the eighteenth century. It was one of the most attractive spots along a stretch of generally flat coastline. Once discovered it was a magnet powerful enough to draw visitors on a difficult and uncomfortable journey on unimproved trackways to a small village with virtually no civilised amenities.

Perception of the resort potential at Weston was one of the factors behind the move to obtain an Act of Parliament for the enclosure of the common lands of the village. Parliamentary enclosure was becoming common among North Somerset parishes by the end of the eighteenth century, the motive generally being a desire for greater agricultural efficiency on the part of leading landowners. Unlike the earlier piecemeal private enclosures it was comprehensive, and ended the medieval commoners' rights over the open land. In 1808 the Pigott family sold a number of the old auster tenements to Richard Parsley, the family's steward at Weston, and William Cox, a tenant of the Pigotts at Brockley, subject to a perpetual ground rent. These two led the initiative and promoted the application for parliamentary enclosure, using as their local agent the Baker family, solicitors, of Aldwick near Blagdon, who had developed something of a speciality in this work; they in turn worked with a specialist lawyer in London. The appointed commissioner, James Staples, began his task in 1810, and the apportionment of about a thousand acres of common land was settled in 1815.

As was the normal practice the commissioner funded the process, which had to be self-financing, by auctioning plots of land. This not only paid for his own expenses but also contributed to the cost of road improvements and bridges, an essential part of a successful enclosure. Mr Staples thought that Weston would spread south and east over the moor, so he chose for auction a number of plots facing the beach south of Watersill Road (Regent Street), as well as some along Watersill Road itself. In 1810 the sea front here consisted of sand dunes which separated the beach from sandy ground behind. Some of the dunes were of considerable height, similar to those which can still be seen towards Uphill by the Golf Course. Sand drifted continually, and there is record of one dwelling, formerly the

SOMERSETSHIRE.

Weston-super-Mare Inclosure.

𝕹otice is hereby given,

That the COMMISSIONERS appointed for carrying into Effect the
Act of Parliament for this Inclosure, will proceed to

𝕾ell (in Fee) by 𝕬uction,

At the House of Joseph Leman, known by the Sign of the NEW INN,
Situate in the Parish of WORLE, in the County of Somerset,

On Monday, the 8th Day of July, 1811,

Between the Hours of FOUR and SIX in the Afternoon,

THE UNDER-MENTIONED

LANDS,

Subject to such Conditions as shall be then produced.

Lot 1.—A Piece of LAND, Part of Weston-super-Mare Moor, containing by Admeasurement
one Acre and an Half, (near the House of the Rev. Mr. Lewis,) bounded Northward by an intended Road, Southward by Lot 3, Eastward by Lot 2, and Westward by the Sea Beach.

Lot 2.—A Piece of LAND, Part of the said Moor, containing by Admeasurement One Acre
and an Half, bounded Northward by the said intended Road, Southward by Lot 3, Eastward by
Part of the said Moor, and Westward by Lot 1.

Lot 3.—A Piece of LAND, Part of the said Moor, containing by Admeasurement Two Acres,
Three Roods, and Ten Perches, bounded Northward by Lots 1 and 2, Southward by Lot 4, Eastward by the said Moor, and Westward by the Sea Beach.

Lot 4.—A Piece of LAND, Part of the said Moor, containing by Admeasurement Five Acres,
bounded Northward by Lot 3, Southward and Eastward by the said Moor, and Westward by the
Sea Beach.

These Lands are put in small Lots, and selected for Sale for the Accommodation of Persons
inclined to build Houses near the Sea and the Village of Weston-super-Mare.

For viewing the Premises, apply to Mr. RICHARD PARSLEY, of Weston-super-Mare, and
for further Particulars and Conditions of Sale, to Mr. JAMES STAPLES, Land-Surveyor, at
his Office, No. 7, Queen-square, Bristol, or to Messrs. SAMUEL and JOHN BAKER,
Solicitors, Blagdon, near Bristol.

RICHARD BISHOP, *Auctioneer.*

By Order of the said Commissioners,

S. BAKER, Clerk.

BROWN, Printer, Mirror Office, Small-Street, Bristol.

home of John Gill, which was eventually demolished by the weight of sand which accumulated over the roof. Four lots were sold in July 1810, at prices ranging between approximately £75 and £150 per acre. Five more lots were sold in August 1811, when Mr Capell of Ashcombe secured a much larger acreage involving the whole of the beach frontage from the present Grand Atlantic Hotel to the site of Severn Road, for £38 per acre. In February 1812 there was a third auction of 36 acres, including the remainder of the beach frontage to the parish boundary where Moorland Road is now and plots along Watersill Road. The development potential of the land was clearly realised. For example, the details of the 1811 auction state:

> These Lands are well calculated for building on, there being excellent Spring water to be found on each Lot at the Depth of Fifteen Feet from the Surface; and the Situation is rendered peculiarly desirable, as no Building can be erected between their Frontage and the Sea.

The land closest to the corner of Watersill Road and the beach became the first to be intensively developed, and St. James' Street, Richmond Street, and Carlton Street made an early appearance on maps of the resort.

Those who became truly private landowners throughout the parish generally as a result of the 1815 award were those who had been the important figures under the old system. The Pigott family retained all the top of the hill and the greater part of the hillside. The Capell (or Caple) family of Ashcombe Manor Farm secured land at Ashcombe and some of the grazing land on the moor. Richard Parsley and William Cox obtained the West Tyning on the hillside and a large tract of land south of the village. This new pattern of land ownership (including smaller awards in the village itself) determined the resort's development, but building proceeded only at a gentle pace for some years to come. The immediate benefits to the major landowners were in terms of farming. Parsley himself appears to have pursued a 'belt and braces' policy during his lifetime. His land on the moor became the Whitecross Estate, and he built Whitecross Lodge to the south of Watersill Road and east of the old Wallclose enclosure: the house can still be discovered behind the Victoria Methodist Church. For some years Parsley used parts of the poor sandy land behind the dunes to grow teazles, which he supplied to the Yorkshire woollen industry (a practice known to have been followed by farmers in other parishes in the area).

Despite this caution, however, Parsley and the other moving spirits clearly had their eyes on development. It should be noted that their entrepreneurial activities followed Weston's emergence as a watering place, and were not the cause of it. Their confidence seems to have been vindicated by the enclosure itself. Out of all the parliamentary enclosures in North Somerset parishes between 1770 and 1830 the selling price of land was higher at Weston than anywhere else, and the economic cost of the process itself, expressed as a percentage, one of the lowest. It is not easy for the imagination to reconcile these commercial considerations with the higher ideals in play during these early years: one perhaps needs to look at Jane Austen's *Sanditon*, unfinished on her death in 1817, which describes a similar stage in the growth of a fictional seaside resort.

Parsley and Cox were partners in another major initiative when they joined with James Capell and a Mr Fry to build the resort's first hotel. It became the Royal Hotel in later years, and is now the Berni Royal in South Parade. We see it today with the extensions and new façade that were added in the 1840s, but a study of the roofline reveals something of the building history. The part nearest Knightstone Road to the north is the original hotel. James Needham was the first tenant, but he was apparently unable to attract enough custom, as the hotel closed and its contents were auctioned in 1811. It reopened in 1814 under the management of Mrs Fry. The stables were built in 1820, the year after Weston's second hotel, The Bath, had opened in the new South Parade; it is now The Imperial. The Plough Hotel was opened in High Street in 1822, so evidently within the decade following Parliamentary enclosure business had considerably increased.

Coaches arriving in Weston had completed a difficult and uncomfortable journey, for the village was still isolated in the early years of the nineteenth century and none of the eighteenth century turnpike roads which formed a network around Bristol came anywhere near it. The usual route from Bristol was down the present A38 to Churchill, then to Banwell and Locking Head, and across the low ridge to Worle. The final stretch involved climbing the hill at Worle and following the Bristol Road along the slope, to descend into Weston at The Grove and the top of High Street. This route was largely superseded from about 1818 by the route through Congresbury, the present A371. Enclosure of Wick St. Lawrence and Puxton (1809 and 1814–16) led to upgrading of the rough country lanes and tracks between Congresbury and Worle, and the Congresbury Drainage Act (1819) alleviated the regular flooding along this route. In 1814 a limited coach service between Bristol and Weston began, and became a regular service within a few years. Dr Bryan Brown has analysed coaching records for this period. The coach service carried increasing numbers of passengers until the coming of the railway in 1841.

As well as passengers, goods had to be brought to the resort to supply staying visitors and guests. Weston had no shop – the nearest was at Worle at the top of The Scaurs, Gunnings Stores, which only recently closed, on Manchester Square. This was the retail centre for all the local villages. Beer for the hotel had to be brought to Weston by handcart from the Worle Brewery. A bell would be rung to announce that beer was available! In 1806 Messrs Stabbins and Hill had begun a carrier service in the summer, using waggons, but this

Gunnings Stores in Manchester Square, Worle at the top of The Scaurs. Until the nineteenth century local villages were largely self-sufficient and this was the only shop in the district.

was short-lived. However in 1811 John Harse revived the service with success. By 1818 he was advertising a post-chaise hiring service as well, and other competitors were soon vying with him. The establishment of a communications and transport network, and the removal of Weston's virtual isolation from the wider world (especially during winter) was a major factor in the resort's increasing popularity.

Thomas Turner, writing in 1815, reported that 'Weston is a very small village, consisting, I imagine, of not more than 30 houses; the majority of these are new, indeed, I may say built within the past 10 years'. The enclosure award of the same year opened the way for further building. In 1821 there were said to be 126 houses, and in 1829 250, of which 150 were lodging houses. Prices ranged between two and six guineas per week. South Parade had been built, and there were a number of 'gentleman's residences' which ringed the old village. Isaac Jacobs, a Bristol glass merchant, built Belvedere facing Beach Road, and next door was Sidmouth House (both were replaced by the Bus Station). Claremont Lodge was built near Anchor Head. Devonshire Cottage (now part of the Chairman's Choice by Manilla Crescent); Highcliffe Lodge in Highbury Road; Wellington Place; Sea View and Belle View (in High Street opposite the Italian Gardens); Weston Hill Cottage (a short way up the Bristol Road); and Vale Cottage at the bottom of Bristol Road, next to the YMCA which was its 'twin' and originally looked very similar, were all built in these years. Weston was 'now a fashionable summer retreat' as the first Guide of 1822, published by John Chilcott of Bristol, declared.

These early buildings were fairly small, simple two-storey dwellings, built of rubble with stucco rendering. They fitted well into the pastoral and low-key character of the new resort, which continued to rely on its natural attractions and the virtues of sea bathing. The elderly Mrs Piozzi, better known as Dr. Johnson's friend Mrs Thrale, wrote from Weston in 1819:

The Breezes here are most salubrious; no land nearer than North America, when we look along the Channel: and 'tis said that Sebastian Cabot used to stand where I sit now and meditate his future Discoveries of Newfoundland. Who would be living in Bath now? . . . We have swarms of Babies here, and some bathe good humouredly enough while others scream and shriek as if they were going to execution . . .

Going into the sea was still a frightening experience for many adults too, and attendants, such as the redoubtable Betty Mugglesworth, were on hand to help the nervous and to chase away any men spying on the ladies. Canvas awnings were erected at the original ladies' bathing place at Anchor Head. When the Hotel opened it boasted the first bathing machine in the village: a changing room on wheels, drawn by a horse into the water, where the modest bather descended steps into the waves. Machines multiplied along the main bay, and continued in use until the beginning of the twentieth century.

Sea bathing was only one of a range of treatments at Weston which, soon after the Enclosure Award, began to be recommended by doctors at Bath and elsewhere. Complex medical regimens were prescribed, including the drinking of sea water. Several baths were established in the resort, the foremost being on Knightstone Island. A bath house and pool were opened here in 1822 by Mr Howe of Bristol, and rented by Benjamin Atwell. The Guide of 1822 made much of the treatments available:

> The bathing establishment consists of a spacious open air swimming bath, plunging and warm baths, either medicated with sulphur, iodine, chlorine or otherwise. The necessary apparatus is

The Bath House on Knightstone Island.

also provided for the administration of the douche, and the superintendant has been instructed in the process of shampooing.

The next owner, the Revd Thomas Pruen, built a low causeway to the island in place of the shingle path, as well as an open air pool fed by the tide. A few years later Dr Edward Long Fox, an influential physician from Brislington near Bristol, spent £20,000 on new facilities. Lodging houses for patients taking 'the cure' were built on the island, and a new bath house in about 1830, which can still be seen. There were other baths in Weston, such as Mrs Gill's in Somerset Place, although these were less elaborate.

Mr Pruen had built a low pier at Knightstone, the traditional anchorage for local fishermen, some of whom were starting to offer their boats for pleasure trips. The 1822 Guide mentions only two pleasure boats, but in 1829 John Rutter's *Westonian Guide* indicates that the number has grown.

> The Weston pleasure and fishing boats are well built and of a good class. They are accounted to be good sea boats of a sufficient size comfortably to accommodate a considerable number of persons,

The view from Knightstone Causeway in 1829, showing bathing machines in attendance and the Hotel on the right.

but mostly without a deck. They are manned by careful and experienced boatmen, who are remarkably civil and attentive and who generally charge 10s 6d for a day's sail, for a party, or 1s for each. The usual place for embarking is at the small pier at Knightstone, but the shore is so flat that the tide rapidly retreats from this spot. At the Anchor Head slip parties may embark or land three hours earlier than at Knightstone.

Steamers began to call occasionally at Weston. Bell's *Comet*, the first commercially viable steam packet in European waters, was built in 1812, and steamers made their appearance early in the Bristol Channel because of the importance of the Port of Bristol. The *Duke of Argyle*, built at Port Glasgow the year before, was the first to ply the open waters of the region in 1815, and regular packet services in the Bristol and St. George's Channels were begun in 1821. Three years later the *Lady Rodney* was the first locally owned packet to run excursions, from Bristol to Flat Holm and Barry Island, and the following year Weston was included in the itinerary. Trips around the Holms were very popular, but the steamer boom did not begin until the 1840s, when the railways were established.

In 1824, after three years of discussion, the old church of St

The new parish church in 1824, incorporating the medieval chancel which was not rebuilt until 1837. The Glebe House is between the church and Grove House.

John's was rebuilt. It had been in a poor state for some years. George Bennett wrote in 1804:

> The roof and windows of the Church and Chancel are in a bad state of repair; one window in particular on the North side of the Chancel I observed to be much broken, and where the glass was wanting, its place supplied by bundles of hay.

The old chancel remained for some years after 1824, but a new nave and improved tower changed the church into a place of worship deemed more fitting and commodious for the resort's fashionable visitors. A gift of £1000 from Wadham Pigott made the work possible, one of his last charitable acts before his death. The new squire, John Hugh Smyth Pigott, persevered with the planting of the hillside as a game reserve in the 1820s, thus creating Weston Woods, which were to mature into a fine backdrop for the Victorian town. Gate lodges were built at the entrances, and two of these can still be seen (at the Kewstoke end of the Toll Road and on the hilltop by the entrance from Worlebury Hill Road). The woods were thrown open to the public in the 1850s. John Hugh also enlarged Grove House considerably, both to accommodate his own family (he had ten

The Assembly Rooms were built at the west end of Regent Street in 1826 and now form part of the Beach Hotel.

children) and numerous guests; the surviving section is the coach house from this period.

By the end of the 1820s there was a low wall and gravelled promenade from Knightstone to Regent Street. Weston was a mixture of town and village, both in terms of physical changes and of attitudes. The encounters between genteel visitors from the polite world and villagers who had grown up in a remote and isolated part of North Somerset could give rise to amusement and disgust – on both sides. This is well caught by Charlotte Wilson in her account of a visit made from Bath, on medical advice, in 1826. There were no proper lodgings to be had, so she stayed with Farmer King and his family in the old farmhouse in Meadow Lane. The family had sent their best furniture to a new

Thic Table wants only zome Wood or Zstones put under the Legs, and then he wull zstand zstraight.

The Worms ha'e yeaten the Voot off he.

The Legs o' thic Chair ha'e been zo vor years. Doan't lean back in he, or you'll vall.

CANDLE 16 TO THE POUND

Did ye never zee zuch zmall Candles bevore? I call him a big one. What we burn are vour -and- twenty to the Pound.

I uze he vor a Roling Pin when I make a Pie.

Thic Crime Jug has lost the Handle, zo has the Coffee Pot. – Ye must lay hold of he at the top wi' a great lump of Rag when ye pours the Coffee out.

Charlotte Wilson's version of the local dialect and some of the farmhouse utensils.

36

Charlotte Wilson's sketch of the Old Farm House, 1826. It stood near Meadow Lane.

lodging house they had built elsewhere in the village. Charlotte Wilson's narrative is meant to be amusing, but it also captures the 'culture shock' of the local farming family and the fashionable London visitor who likes sketching the local scenery. Her sketches and renderings of the local dialect are a useful record, and a valuable corrective to the inevitable image-building of the early guidebooks.

WHAT TO SEE

- Glebe House, east of St. John's: Weston's oldest house, with additions and remodelled façade from the early nineteenth century.

- Grove House in Grove Park: stable block of the 1830s.

- Leeves' Cottage ('The Old Thatched Cottage'), Knightstone Road.

- Berni Royal (formerly Royal Hotel) and the Imperial Hotel, South Parade.

- Early houses: South Parade; Vale Cottage and Weston Hill Cottage, Lower Bristol Road; Highcliffe Lodge, Highbury Road; Whitecross Lodge, behind Methodist Church, Station Road.

- St. John's: nave and tower.

- Bath House, Knightstone.

37

Building Victorian Weston

The pace of development quickened within a few years of the arrival of Brunel's broad gauge railway in 1841. Ironically, only just before this the road system had been upgraded, an Act of Parliament of 1840 enabling a Turnpike Trust to improve existing lanes and build new sections of road on the flat land between Weston and Worle. This created an alternative way into Weston to the old hillside route, joining the Watersill Road, the present Locking Road and A371. The Trust was the second last body of its kind in the country, although it continued to collect tolls until the 1880s.

Weston was one of the first seaside resorts to enjoy a rail connexion, and thus became accessible to visitors from farther afield. Brunel himself stayed at Swiss Villa, a detached mansion in large grounds, which stood where Trevelyan Road is today, while this section of the Bristol and Exeter line was being constructed across the Northmarsh. It is said that the original proposal to bring the main line closer to the town was opposed by leading local landowners. The main line passed Weston by, and a branch line was built from 'Wessun Junction' to the first station, which stood where the Floral Clock now is in Regent Street. Winterstoke Road perpetuates the course of the branch

A drawing by Raymond Dwerryhouse of the first railway station, which was at the west end of Alexandra Parade on the site of the Floral Clock.

line, along which, in the early years, carriages were drawn by horses. The branch line acquired its own steam engines to replace the horses in 1851. The Railway Hotel (now Quantocks) was immediately to the west of the station.

Weston's population when the railway arrived was about 2000 and building had not spread far beyond the area of the old village, as the 1838 Tithe Map reveals. The area of the Beach Road plots had been consolidated, and there was building activity by the beach near Leeves' Cottage. Victoria Buildings, as the name suggests, were new, and the two southerly houses of the seven in the terrace still reveal the character of the originals: simple, small, two-storey properties in the Georgian tradition, with rendered walls, the roofs hidden by parapets, relying upon proportion for their pleasing effect. In West Lane itself, on the other side of Leeves' Cottage, Henry Davies was building the two Beachfield Villas, still to be seen with later additions. These too strike us as modest (apart from the porticoes), but it is recorded

The town seen from the southern ramparts of the hillfort in the 1850s. Royal Crescent appears behind the tower of the Villa Rosa. The impact of this new scale of building can be readily appreciated. Note the small quarry, with its own lime kiln, in the foreground.

that Davies was asked by the Rector of Weston, from whom he had acquired this portion of the Glebe land, whether there would be sufficient demand for such spacious premises. Yet within a few years of the railway's arrival Davies was building much grander properties. He was a solicitor, who became Clerk to the new Board of Commissioners in 1842, and was a leading figure among the new generation of entrepreneurs.

Davies pioneered a still more ambitious concept which was to give Weston some of its most impressive domestic architecture during the following quarter of a century, although the building of more modest houses still continued after 1841, as at Albert Buildings, 1843, or Wadham Street, begun 1846. He initially concentrated his activity in the area between Victoria Buildings and Lower Church Road, which had been built in 1826 to replace the old path to the church. Royal Crescent was begun in 1847, with giant arches in the Roman style. Facing it across ornamental gardens was Greenfield Place, while in Lower Church Road itself, on former Glebe land, was Oriel Terrace, originally known as East Terrace. South Terrace, round the corner, repeats the style on a smaller scale. By the early 1850s Davies had set a new standard of building for the resort. It was

Ellenborough Crescent, the largest of the new prestige developments of the middle years of the nineteenth century. *Woodspring Museum.*

not merely that his crescent and terraces were faced with Bath stone, brought by the new railway; these new buildings, as the name of Royal Crescent signifies, also looked to the architectural tradition of Bath as a role model. They are single designs echoing the grandeur of palaces, within which the individual houses defer to the whole.

On the death of Richard Parsley in 1846, Henry Davies and Joseph Whereat, a stationer, bookseller, newspaper publisher and proprietor of the Assembly Rooms, acquired the Whitecross Estate which stretched across the moor to Uphill. In 1855 they began the biggest 'set piece' development in the Bath tradition yet seen in the resort: Ellenborough Crescent, looking across the length of Ellenborough Park to the sea. This new prestige development was named after Lord Ellenborough, former Governor-General of India and First Lord of the Admiralty, whose brother, Archdeacon Law, was Rector of Weston. Others adopted this bold approach. The twin halves of Manilla Crescent, facing Glentworth Bay, were built in 1851, and the tradition continued into the next decade with Claremont Crescent, which replaced Claremont Lodge above Anchor Head, and the two Atlantic Terraces, an audacious concept flanking Holy Trinity Church.

Each one of these terrace or crescent houses was itself quite large (today they make three or four flats), and they are indicative of a new found confidence in the resort, which was beginning to benefit through the railway link from the high noon of Victorian prosperity. Wealth, and with it leisure habits, was more widely spread, reaching down the social scale to the professional, trading and manufacturing classes who formed the upper middle class. Thus the resort reflected indirectly Britain's early lead in industrial production and export. Census returns show that many occupants of the new buildings were 'fund holders' living off private incomes and investments. The railway meant that businessmen could live at Weston without being cut off from their offices or factories. Joseph Whereat observed in his *Weston Gazette* in 1845:

> Weston-super-Mare is found to be just at the most convenient distance from Bristol and Bath, in that gentlemen can easily bring their families hither, and come and return by early and late trains without interruption of their normal hours of business.

Terraces from the 1860s. Above, Royal Terrace, with the Royal Hotel on its right, seen across the Hotel Field which later became the Winter Gardens. Below, Atlantic Terrace and Holy Trinity Church, in the district which was known as Cliftonville.

By 1854 there were seven trains daily to Bristol from Weston. Many clergymen lived in the resort, and another significant group were the retired Army and Navy officers who had served the Empire overseas.

The new buildings displayed a truly urban spirit for the first time, and this in turn lent credibility to Weston's pretensions towards becoming a winter resort and a place of all-year-round residence. The resort had attracted a few winter residents in the 1830s, who were seeking a good climate for convalescence. In 1847 Whereat, ever eager to promote the town, was congratulating a group of visitors from Cheltenham who had shown the courage to stay in Weston during the winter months. The 'change of gear' in building is well indicated in the following, from Woods *Excursionist's Guide* of 1855:

> Seven or eight years ago, the Beach, Park Place, Victoria and Albert Buildings, may be said to have comprised the chief ranges of private dwellings and lodging houses. Since that period, an immense impulse has been given to building enterprise. As if by magic, there have sprung up Oriel Terrace, the Crescent, Greenfield Place, Prince's Buildings, Manilla Crescent and Wellington Terrace fronting the hill; together with an almost equal number of streets and houses of less note in different parts of the town. The splendour of many of the buildings just enumerated strikes with surprise the unsuspecting visitor on returning to it, after an absence of many years.

At the same time a second building type was becoming established, which in the long run was to prove the more significant. This was the villa, which embodied a tradition quite different from that of the terrace or crescent where all the residences formed parts of a larger whole. By contrast the villa was private and separate in its own grounds, and answered better to the Victorian middle class ideal. The villa was detached, although even semi-detached houses met the bill almost as well. As the town broke out of its village straitjacket in the years following the railway's arrival, entire new estates of villas were begun, forming new suburbs. The Grove Estate, to the east of The Grove itself, was the first major development on the Smyth Pigott land, begun in the late 1850s. Grove Town above The Boulevard (Southside) was projected in 1860, the year when The Boulevard itself was laid out (influenced, it is said, by the Lord of the Manor's Francophile tastes). This major new avenue was aligned on the spire of Christchurch, begun in 1854, itself the focus of the

Footbridge in The Shrubbery, which linked the grounds of the Villa Rosa across the road that led to the new villas of the Shrubbery Estate.

new Montpelier Estate where building began in 1858. The area around Ellenborough Park was developed with large villas from the 1850s onwards. On the hillside to the west, the grounds of the Villa Rosa (a striking Italianate mansion of the 1830s) were developed as The Shrubbery Estate, and westward again the district around Holy Trinity Church, known as Cliftonville, was begun. South Road began to be built along in the 1860s. The only project of this kind which failed to materialise was the Swiss Villa Estate, to the south of Montpelier; being close neither to the hill nor the sea but only to the new main road and artisans' cottages, it lacked the advantages of setting to compete with the other initiatives.

Setting was important; most of the new estates were, in their early years, separated from the town centre by fields, and they maintained an exclusive air. Their roads were private and sometimes protected by gatekeepers' lodges, which in some cases can still be seen. Each villa had its private garden, soon filled with the shrubs beloved of the Victorians, and several of the estates also had communal gardens for the sole use of the residents (The Shrubbery, Ellenborough Park, Landemann Circus, Eastfield Park). Original plans of these handsome houses reveal a layout calculated for a comfortable life style: not only a lounge, dining room, breakfast room, several bedrooms and 'usual offices', but also a wine cellar, billiard room, or study. Bay windows gave fine views from the principal rooms, which had high ceilings with plaster decoration, and large imposing fireplaces. The villa was designed for restful, secluded and comfortable retirement in leafy surroundings, solid yet stylish and confident: an emblem of Victorian middle class values and aspirations.

In these havens of genteel respectability there were no shops of any kind, and, naturally, no public houses. The villas all had servants' quarters, either in the attics, rear wings, or semi-basements, which can still be identified. The owners were all wealthy enough to employ domestics (the census returns show that most villas had at least two servants living in), and so Weston's population was swelled by a small army of servants, drawn in the main from the surrounding villages. Cooking and heating consumed large quantities of coal, brought in to Knightstone Harbour, and the tall chimney stacks are a prominent feature of the buildings. Goods were delivered by horse or donkey from shops in the town centre. A vast economic gulf separated the wealthy villa residents from the people who lived in the town's working neighbourhoods, yet they were not quite upper class; few of them, for example, had their own carriages, and so only the grandest villas have stabling and a carriage 'sweep' in front of the house. The town had numerous mews from which horses and carriages could be hired when required.

Whereas the terraces and crescents boasted Bath stone façades, Weston's villas soon began to use the better quality carboniferous limestone which was now being produced from the Town Quarry and others in the district. This hard grey stone is actually better suited to withstand the rigours of the coastal climate, and local masons developed great skill in shaping it precisely and exploiting it to the full; in many buildings it was used as ashlar. However the softer Bath stone continued to be used around doors and windows, in quoins, corbels, and for decorative ornament, as it could be cut easily. It was also used for the tops of garden walls and for gate pillars.

West Elevation

← Road to house

South Elevation

N.B. : Pathway to Back door.
The Water drain
to be made in the upper part of the bank

North Elevation

Water drains here & another
overflow
from here to dry pit within bank

← Approximate level of Road to house

East Elevation

46

Chamber-Plan.

Ground Plan.

Architect's drawings for a typical villa built on the Weston hillside. Notice the separate servants' wing and back stairs, making the two sections of the house independent of each other.

47

The roofscape of Weston villadom: looking over Grove Park Road and Queen's Road towards the Mendips. *Howard Smith.*

By the 1860s local limestone and freestone were superseding brick or rubble walls covered with render even in the new working class dwellings which were filling up spaces on the flat land around the town centre; Palmer Street and Alfred Street are good examples. George Street was begun in the 1870s, largely to provide guest and lodging houses. The National Freehold Land Society began building around Clarendon Road in the late 1860s. There was a degree of continuity, in terms of building materials, throughout the town, and working class houses in Weston were sturdy buildings, even though socially they were not always approved of: Rambler complained in 1887 that small tenements were being built everywhere, for rents of £25 or under, and lowering the tone of the resort. The villa itself was capable of adaptation to the needs of lower social groups, and as the century progressed more modest versions of the semi-detached style were being built for the lower middle classes. The process reached working class homes towards the turn of the century, and the style replaced the terraced housing of the older workers' streets. There was a consistency in terms of building materials throughout the town until the First World War.

Estate development was a particular form of residential development, as favoured by many Weston landowners as it was in other towns and cities in Victorian England. Large tracts of land were offered for building, and individual plots were sold or leased subject to strict conditions. These controlled not only the layout of the estate but also the size and type of dwelling to be built, the materials to be used, the completion date and the ultimate price. The system guaranteed that all the houses in an area blended with each other, even though several different builders may have been responsible for them. It also ensured that the 'tone' of the estate was maintained: a matter of fine judgement and estimation of the market. Land could be released gradually, at a rate dictated by the market. The release of land had a great effect on the local economy. This was the form taken by development on the land progressively released by the Smyth Pigott family, who used the unusual system of selling plots subject to a perpetual rent charge. A typical rent charge for a hillside property was, and still is, £10 per annum. This system not only brought in capital but also an income after the land was sold and the houses completed. Estate development in this form also enabled the Smyth Pigott family to ensure a degree of town planning and aesthetic control which was more stringent in many respects than the statutory system we have today, and at no cost to themselves.

The roofscape of working-class Weston: looking south down Palmer Street.

From soon after the mid-point of the nineteenth century effective control of the Smyth Pigott estate at Weston was in the hands of a small network of professional men. The agent was Robert Landemann Jones (after whom Landemann Circus is named), who was born in Barnstaple in 1816. His father was engaged in the China trade and went down with his ship when Jones was a baby. Jones himself ran away to sea when a boy, and apart from a brief period in a solicitor's office he remained on the China coast for eighteen years, being commander and part-owner of his vessel. He returned to England, married in 1847, and took up farming; some of this period he spent at Blagdon, where he no doubt became acquainted with the Baker family, solicitors to the Smyth Pigott estate, and perhaps with the Smyth Pigotts themselves. He took over the management of their estates around 1860 and recouped their profitability. In 1872 Jones told a dinner of the Master Builders at Weston that the estate had built 250 houses in the preceeding ten years, increasing the rent roll by £2500 per annum.

The need to secure a regular income for the estate was underlined by the difficulties into which the then Lord of the Manor, John Hugh Wadham Pigott Smyth Pigott, had run. He seems to have been a difficult character in many ways. It was not merely that he was a lover of Paris who became a convert to Roman Catholicism, endowing the first Roman Catholic church at Weston, St Joseph's; it appears that he also amassed large gambling debts. A trust was established to salvage his affairs. In 1855 there was a mortgage of estate land, including some in Weston and in several villages, to secure £10,000 and interest. Even the Grove House was let for a while, the family moving to a house overlooking Prince Consort Gardens. Jones was a principal figure in redeeming the family fortunes, but relationships between the squire and his agent were often tempestuous. We read in 1861:

> Rumours have been rife during the week, to the effect that Mr R. L. Jones, the agent to John Hugh Smyth Pigott, Esq. . . . had been peremptorily removed from the management of the estates, and that removal had taken place in consequence of certain disclosures, which will in all probability lead to a suit in the Court of Divorce.

Pigott and his wife were the subject of a 'skimmity ride' after his wife, who was much younger than her husband, gave birth to a son in 1860 and there were rumours that the squire was not the child's father. A local rabble paraded past the house above Flagstaff Hill one evening carrying effigies of their luckless victims. The child was Cecil, later Lord of the Manor in his turn, after whom Cecil Road is named.

The naming of roads was itself one of the numerous causes of friction between John Hugh Wadham and the Town Commissioners, who had been established by Act of Parliament as the local government body soon after the coming of the railway. The Board of eighteen members had only limited powers at first, but their role grew commensurately with the reforming legislation passed throughout the Victorian period. The Commissioners tended to include the leading developers and entrepreneurs of the town, whereas John Hugh Wadham was a bastion of the old county ruling class. He was taken to task by the Commissioners in 1870 for putting up name plates in the new roads without their permission. The letter columns in the local press resounded with mutual accusation. One writer described the Lord of the Manor as 'a useless member of the community'. John Hugh Wadham in turn abused the Commissioners: 'more than half of them being only colonists and squatters on my manor, and the other half parvenus and upstarts'. Of one particular correspondent he said that 'he is not worthy to clean my servant's boots'. On another occasion the squire was outraged when the Commissioners installed a public seat by the Toll Road to Kewstoke. He had his men pull it up and deposit it outside the Town Hall. These upsets cannot have made the harmonious development of the resort easy during the boom years.

A fashionable watering place in the nineteenth century was not expected to have any industry. Its function was to offer an escape, for those who could afford it, from the grime, pollution, and ugliness that disfigured many of the inland towns and cities which had made Britain into 'the workshop of the world'. For working people in Weston and the surrounding villages employment prospects were therefore limited to trade and service, as well as work on the farms and market gardens which supplied the fashionable visitors and residents with the necessities of life. Apart from this, Weston was not an industrial town, and did not become one to any significant extent until well into the present century.

The one exception in Victorian Weston was the building industry itself. Census returns reveal a small army of building

Above, a rare view of construction taking place: the left half of Manilla Crescent being built in 1851, with Glentworth Hall on the right. Below, the same view towards the end of the nineteenth century, and, right, today.

tradesmen and their labourers, in a town where the main
industrial activity for two generations was building the town
itself: masons, bricklayers, plasterers, carpenters, painters,
plumbers, slaters and tilers. Their work was often seasonal.
Buildings in the course of construction are not something which
figures much in the annals of the resort, although it must have
been difficult to turn a corner without seeing a building site. It
was not the type of scene which Victorians photographed or
described, but the buildings we see enable us to deduce the level
of activity in an age when buildings were mainly constructed by
hand, even though mass production techniques were beginning
to make an appearance.

Vast quantities of stone were taken from the Town Quarry,
which backs onto Weston Woods at the top of Queen's Road and
which developed from the village gravel pit. The Enclosure Act
enshrined the rights of owners of 'old auster or ancient tenements' to take stone for building or the repair of roads. Methods
of working changed little over the years. Stone-getters normally
worked in small gangs, and each gang was responsible for its
own blasting, breaking, and haulage within the quarry. The
method of boring for the shot-holes was to 'jump the holes
down', working a rod up and down until the hole was about six
feet deep. Rows of holes were drilled two or three feet apart, and

A gang at the quarry face, at the beginning of this century.

then filled with charge and a fuse cable. The resulting explosion might lift out between ten and thirty tons of stone. Conditions in the quarry were very harsh. The 'roads' to the quarry face were simply two long heaps of rubbish, and the horses often fell between the heaps as they dragged the carts along.

Mechanisation did not make its appearance until the later years of the century. In 1880 a stone-breaker and a ten ton steam roller were purchased by the Commissioners, and soon afterwards a machine for making tarmacadam was installed. Steam power made drilling and crushing easier, as well as eventually improving haulage, but the quarry was still a dangerous place. Its proximity to some of the most prestigious villas in the town was an embarrassment. Blasting sometimes sent stone into the leafy retreats of leading residents, who in 1879 petitioned the Commissioners to enforce tighter controls. At a meeting one of the Commissioners himself produced a stone that had come through his window while he was shaving. However the Commissioners were advised that, as the quarry had preceded the houses, there was little that could be done. If the local gentry suffered inconvenience the quarrymen themselves faced constant danger and even death in blasting accidents. For example, in February 1886 a quarryman named Edward Vile, who lived in Palmer Street, died after a charge exploded late; he left a widow and two children.

Most of the hard carboniferous limestone is grey in colour, but quantities of pink stone, stained through the presence of iron, were also found and were in great demand for ornamental purposes, although the pink stone is not as durable as the grey. Occasionally houses were built entirely from pink stone, after the fashion of the Villa Rosa in The Shrubbery. There were many other small quarries along the hillside, some of which now form the gardens of villas built from the stone won on the site. Towards the end of the century Milton Quarry was developed and was later given modern bottle kilns for lime burning, by Henry Butt, a self-made local businessman. The Windsor Castle at Milton was originally called the Mason's Arms because its trade was drawn from the local quarrymen.

Stone masons at the top of their trade were able to dress the

Building the road at Milton Hill.

hard local stone so precisely that in many buildings it was used as ashlar, although more often it was laid random. Some of the 'old-timers' could dress the stone with a sledgehammer ready to go straight into a wall. Their skills were in such demand in the rapidly growing resort that they felt able to strike in 1858, at the height of the first building boom; in April between 100 and 150 masons and their labourers were on strike. The masons, who earned £1 a week, were demanding two shillings a week more and a half hour a day less work, but the master builders wanted to cut wages by two shillings and keep the same hours. The strike lasted for several weeks and must have been an unprecedented example of organised militancy in the town. An increase of one shilling a week was eventually agreed.

Many other building materials were produced locally. Holm sand, dredged up in the deep water shipping route in the Bristol Channel and taken to Bristol to be purified of salt, was sold to the building trade. The by-products of local quarries were also used. Gravel was produced in large quantities for roads and paths, that from Worle Quarry at the east end of the hill being regarded as the best because it stayed clean and matched the colour of the building stone. There were numerous lime kilns in the area, such as the one recently restored at Uphill near the boatyard. Coal dust and small coal was used to burn stone rubble loaded into the top of the kiln, and the resulting burnt lime was raked out of a smaller opening below; this was used both on the land and in lime mortar. Kilns were kept burning for weeks at a time, being topped up with alternate layers of coal and stone, and the draught controlled by openings in a 'lean-to' built against the side over the lower opening.

Local potteries were major suppliers to the building trade. William Wilcox had opened a pottery in Locking Road by 1836, and a second site was in operation a few years later, which was taken over in 1847 by Charles Phillips, an illiterate local man who manufactured flower pots as well as bricks and tiles. His products won an honourable mention at the Great Exhibition of 1851, and the venture became the 'Royal Potteries' after winning the contract to supply the royal parks. A wide range of garden urns and other ornamental pieces was developed alongside the more routine articles. By the 1880s, when flower pot production reached 1½ million a year, the potteries were rated the largest single source of production in England.

The clay was generally dug in the autumn, and spread out and

56

The pottery in Locking Road during the 1870s.

left to weather until spring. It was then turned several times and put through a pug-mill and wedged to remove air bubbles. Clay for bricks was mixed with sand to prevent shrinkage and to encourage the bricks to fire all the way through. Brick clay was either cut with wire or pressed into wooden moulds, and the tools were also of wood, often made by the men themselves. The moulds were always slightly larger than the required size of the finished article, to allow for shrinkage during firing. In the kilns, of which there were six eventually, the bricks were stacked around the walls and the flower pots 'nested' in the middle. One can still see many examples of the pottery's tiles and ridge tiles on local houses, their cheerful orange-red colour making a happy contrast with the local stone. The business was bought by John Matthews in 1871, and was taken over by Conway Warne in 1884. Much of the work was seasonal, and demand fluctuated with the fortunes of the building industry; at one point the venture was rescued from bankruptcy and relaunched by the Pigott estate, which had a vested interest in the local building market.

The claypits on the Northmarsh near Locking Road, just east of Ashcombe Road, filled with water and were popular with small boys for fishing. When the water froze in winter they were used as skating rinks, not only during the daytime but also at night, when people skated by torchlight. Sometimes the town band was hired to enliven proceedings and there would be hot coffee, tea and other refreshments. Unemployed men would earn money fixing skates for the ladies and gentlemen. By 1900 the old potteries site was worked out. Building had spread out of town to reach its limits, sending up the price of land and making expansion of the site uneconomic. A new site at Langford Road was brought into operation. Brick production boomed for a while, but by the 1930s it was the humble flower pot that was the mainstay of the business. Plastic pots eventually brought it to an end, and the firm went into voluntary liquidation in 1961.

The town had its own sawmills in Meadow Street, and its own iron foundry, which began as Pond's in 1840 but was taken over by Hillman's in 1850 and survived until 1962. The foundry was at the south-east corner of Richmond Street and produced gates, railings, drainpipes and covers, lamp posts and street name plates, many of which can still be seen. Good communications made the import of some materials relatively easy, the most notable being Welsh slate and Bath stone. The blue or violet tints

Hans Fowler Price, 'the doyen of the architectural profession at Weston'.
Woodspring Museum

of roof slates mingled with local pottery tiles to give the hillside town an attractive roofscape, while honey-coloured Bath stone, the prestige building material of the time, came by rail from its source only thirty miles away. In *The Fashionable Stone* Kenneth Hudson reproduces the price list for delivered Bath stone published in 1856 by Randell and Saunders, a leading firm of quarry owners at Coombe Down, Corsham Down and Box Hill: the prices for delivery to Weston are among the cheapest quoted for anywhere in the country and show the added advantage which developers of this 'stone town' enjoyed.

Many local builders were their own architects or relied upon the pattern books for fashionable villas which were widely available. Weston's presiding architectural genius was Hans Fowler Price, who established his practice in Weston at about the same time that Jones took over management of the Pigott estates and worked closely with him. Price was born in 1835 at Langford near Weston, and was articled to Thomas Denville Barry of Liverpool. He set up practice at 5 High Street in 1860, living at 5 Victoria Villas, three doors away from Samuel Baker of the family firm of solicitors which acted for the Pigott estates. In 1862 Price married Baker's sister Jane, and the couple lived for nearly thirty years at 'Tyn-y-Coed' in Hill Road. The Bakers' role in running the manor estate was considerable, and the connexion helped Price to become consulting architect for the Pigott developments. He designed scores of the villas that filled Jones' new suburbs, varying the basic formula with individual touches and decorative details so that each property had its own character and identity. His role in the team that developed the Pigott land was crucial in setting the tone of the growing watering place.

The railway had opened the way for the building boom, and the town's population expanded rapidly. From just over 2000 in 1841 it doubled to just over 4000 in 1851 and then doubled again to just over 8000 in 1861. Thereafter it climbed steadily to reach over 18,000 at the end of the century. It was not long before the original station and branch line were proving inadequate to cope with the increased traffic in and out of the resort. In 1855 the *Weston Gazette* stated that the town had outgrown the existing facilities. A second station was opened in 1866 on the site now occupied by the new Tesco store next to the Odeon. It was much larger, with a long excursion platform and a goods shed. Passengers alighted in front of the Town Hall and the Bristol and Exeter

Weston-super-Mare at the time of the coming of the railway, based on the Tithe Map of 1838.

public house (now the Town Crier) at the end of Oxford Street, but they had still to travel along the old branch line. In 1875 this was converted to mixed gauge, and the following year the Bristol and Exeter Railway Company was absorbed into the Great Western. In 1878 Brunel's old broad gauge finally disappeared and the branch was standard gauge only. The Great Western was keen to link Weston to the main line by a loop, and work began on the present loopline in 1882. When it was completed two years later Weston's present station was opened, the town's third. Much of the second station survived as the goods station, and there was now an excursion platform nearly a quarter of a mile long stretching from Alexandra Parade towards the Gas Works. This complex track layout remained in use for nearly eighty years. The goods station closed in 1960, and the excursion platform was demolished in 1967. More recent proposals to close

Weston-super-Mare when the third railway station was built, based on the Ordnance Survey of 1886.

or downgrade the station in favour of a new one on the main line itself have been successfully resisted so far, but in an era of continuing retrenchment for the national railway network the threat of this sort of rationalisation remains a cause for local anxiety.

Weston's three railway stations, and the track layout after the third station and the loopline had been built.

1. 1841
2. 1866
3. 1884

WHAT TO SEE

● Royal Crescent; Greenfield Place; Oriel Terrace, Lower Church Road.

● Ellenborough Crescent.

● Atlantic Terraces, Atlantic Road.

● Villas: the hillside between Prince Consort Gardens and Eastfield Park; the Walliscote Road area.

● Estate development and communal gardens: The Shrubbery, Landemann Circus, Eastfield Park, Ellenborough Park.

● Workers' terraces in the Meadow Street area.

● Town Quarry, South Road; Uphill Quarry and lime kiln.

● Potteries display in Woodspring Museum, Burlington Street.

● Railway Station: the third station, built in the 1880s.

Public Works

House building surged ahead in the years following the railway's arrival, but other developments were also necessary to support the relaxed life style of the new residents and visitors. A basic infrastructure was created using the new technology and engineering skills of the age to provide the often unseen services which the imposing new residences required in order to function. Other amenities and services appeared gradually as the town organised itself and its citizens acquired the full spectrum of facilities that make up a town in the fullest sense of the word. Sometimes enterprising individuals filled a gap; at other times new forms of public organisation emerged to meet local needs. It should be remembered that during this period social and

The main section of High Street, looking south, with Osterley Buildings on the right.

economic change was dominated by a utilitarian ethos which reflected the manufacturing and commercial interests that were rising in the country generally. It was a time of *laissez-faire*. The new entrepreneurs distrusted public legislation, believed government interference should be kept to a minimum nationally and locally, and trusted to the unregulated efforts of individuals to achieve harmonious economic order and well-being.

Shops naturally appeared as housing spread. There had been none in the village, and the first in the young resort was Cornelius Hancock's in The Street, which became High Street, the principal shopping street in the town; its curving line is still a reminder of village days. At first extensions were thrown out over the front gardens of dwelling houses, but increasing rebuilding produced more adequate shop premises, many of which we can see today. In 1845 Joseph Whereat observed that in Weston 'the past few years have made many alterations to the number and neatness of its shops'. By the late 1850s High Street had over forty shops, half the total of the town. The premises of Owen Owen date from this period. In 1871 the terrace of Osterley Buildings containing eleven shops was built on the site of Spring Cottage, on the west side running down from the Italian Gardens. High Street was not completely built up because covenants enjoyed by early lodging houses guaranteed their open views to the beach; hence the Italian Gardens area remained a field belonging to the Royal Hotel, and visitors to the best shops passed allotments and cattle grazing in the heart of town.

Later Victorian shops had ornate fronts, with handsome fascias and ornamental woodwork. Plate glass windows became common, allowing elaborate displays of goods. There was usually a stall-riser on which the window sill rested, and the design of shopfronts was of a piece with the architecture, embodying quality and reliability. Shops had gas lighting, and it was normal for them to stay open until eight or nine o'clock in the evening. Most shops were locally owned.

Regent Street and St James' Street were other early shopping streets, reflecting the early date of building in that area following the Enclosure Act. At the sea front end of Regent Street was Whereat's Reading Room and Assembly Rooms, an important institution for those with time on their hands and cultural pretensions. The original building of 1826 is now incorporated into the Beach Hotel opposite the Grand Pier. Whereat was another important figure who profited from the post-railway

Regent Street in the middle of the nineteenth century, looking towards the sea, with the Wesleyan Church on the left at the corner of St James' Street. Below, the same view today.

boom, the publisher of the town's first newspaper, founded in 1845. New Assembly Rooms were built by a limited company of townspeople in 1858 at the corner of West Street and High Street, a casualty of bomb damage in the Second World War.

St James' Street was considered by some to be as important as High Street in the early years of the town, and as it has been less extensively redeveloped it gives a better feeling of the scale and character of the town centre at this time. Rufus Palmer, whose father had come to the town from Lympsham in 1830 and who eventually started a bootmaking business, described his childhood memories of the street in his autobiography. He was born in 1846, and the family's shop was Number 12. Here Rufus grew up with his six brothers and sisters and his parents, 'not only highly respectable, but pious and Godfearing Persons'.

> In those days plate glass had not been introduced. Our shop front consisted of about a dozen squares of glass, about 24 ins. by 18 ins., enclosing a window-board whereon was displayed a few samples of my father's wares, a pair of top boots – top boots were generally worn in those days by the gentry – various other boots and shoes and a pair or two of worked slippers.

One of young Palmer's best friends was Albert King, whose father kept the White Lion public house across the street (the lion is still over the door), and nearby in the street were Johnny Walker's leather and grindery shop, Cole's fishmonger's and fruiterer's business, and Bradbury's Pawnbroking Establishment.

The junction of Regent Street, High Street and Meadow Street had been the site of the village green, a small area now the site of the Midland Bank. It remained in many respects the hub of community life, recalled in its old name of Gossip Corner. Present Westonians remember it by its later name of Big Lamp Corner, after the gas lamp that stood here. This was the scene of New Year celebrations and the place to meet on summer evenings. There was never a planned central open space in the Victorian town centre befitting its size: town planning functions were effectively divided between the Pigott estate, confined through the pattern of land ownership to areas away from the centre, and the Commissioners, whose powers were very limited during the early years when the outlines of the town centre were taking shape. So, while the sea front was the place for promenading, Gossip Corner remained the meeting place for local

Looking north up the main section of High Street in 1861. The spire denotes the Independent Church of 1858, now Woolworths. Below, the same view today.

67

The northern section of High Street, looking towards Grove Park. On the right is the terrace designed by Hans Price which incorporated the entrance to the Market (now the site of The Playhouse).

working people. To the south was the first working class area, now largely redeveloped. To the east was the second area of workers' streets, opening off Meadow Street, built during the 1850s and 1860s. This area survives intact, and one can still explore a district which housed hundreds of working families in simple terraced dwellings, with workshops and small businesses hidden behind. The shops in Meadow Street – still the most important 'local' shopping street – served this tightly knit community.

More prestigious commercial buildings appeared later in the century, and Hans Price designed several, including Magdala Buildings (1869) on the corner opposite the Odeon Cinema, and the richly ornamented terrace on the east side of North High Street; the latter incorporated a new façade for the Market (now the Playhouse), which had originally been out of doors, moved into its first building here in 1827, was rebuilt in 1858, and was redesigned by Price in 1900. The northern part of the town centre attracted many of the superior businesses, and also the banks. There was one at each end of South Terrace: Stuckey's Bank,

The Boulevard, looking east from Waterloo Street.

where the National Westminster is now, and a branch of the Wiltshire and Dorset where Lloyds is today. Waterloo Street was opened up in 1860 with the demolition of Waterloo Cottage and acquired some handsome premises connecting the town centre with The Boulevard, including Price's own offices at Number 28, still occupied by his firm's descendants.

In 1812 letters had been delivered once a week by a man on a donkey; ten years later the resort was a penny post from Bristol. A Stamp Office opened in 1844, and the first Post Office was established at 5 Somerset Place, High Street in 1855. In 1875 the Post Office moved to a site next to the Market House Inn, and now occupied by Julian Flook's; there were stables for the Post Office reached from Old Post Office Lane. In 1899 a new General Post Office opened overlooking the Hotel Field on the site of the former Veranda House. Another move is planned shortly.

As the town grew rapidly in the middle years of the century it drew in traders from far afield. Taking Wadham Street as an example, the 1851 census shows it to have contained a druggist from Devon, a tea dealer from Worcester, a plasterer from Hereford, a brewer from Wiltshire, a dressmaker from Devon, a chairman from North Petherton, a grocer from Butcombe and a tailor from Spaxton.

Weston's Commissioners had only limited scope for action in their early years: street lighting, drainage, paving and 'watching' (organising the watch) were their only powers, and Alfred Street was the eastern limit of their jurisdiction. They could raise a rate, which was set at ninepence in the pound in the first years. One of the Commissioners' first measures was to organise the widening of High Street, where there had hardly been room for two carriages to pass.

Drainage and sewage constantly exercised the minds of Weston's leaders. It was not simply the practical necessity of catering for a rapidly increasing number of private dwellings that made this an early priority of local government in the town. A watering place was jealous of its reputation as a healthy resort for invalids and hypochondriacs, in an age when conditions were often appalling in inland towns and cities and epidemics were a constant threat. There is a record of a cholera epidemic at Weston as early as 1831. The young town simply took advantage of the system of ditches or rhynes that criss-crossed the moor and found their way into the Uphill Great Rhyne, the Uphill Pill and the Axe; or properties relied upon cess pits. In 1842 the Commissioners accepted a tender from Benjamin Brice for building the first proper sewers in the town. In 1850 there were complaints about the sewage in the Uphill Rhyne, and the following year the Commissioners held a competition for proposals to overcome the nuisance and the inadequacies of the system: a sewer was laid from Milton Road along Ashcombe Road to disinfecting works in Drove Road in 1856.

The fluctuating population of a resort was part of the problem. The sudden arrival of thousands of visitors put an enormous strain on the services and sewage seeped from the open rhynes into wells. Although such incidents were not reported, there is evidence that outbreaks of typhoid and cholera continued. Fevers and deaths as a result of pollution were fairly common, especially among the poorer classes. Weston had a healthy reputation, and certainly was healthier than many places, but standards are relative. There was still nervousness about anything that might undermine the salubrious image. One visitor wrote in 1860 complaining at the loss of two daughters in as many weeks through illness: his letter (preserved in Woodspring Central Library) is the more telling because it has a tone of only mild reproof, reminiscent of Lady Bracknell, suggesting that one might perhaps expect to lose one child but that to lose two through disease was a poor reflection on the town.

In 1865 Joseph Bazalgette was retained to propose a new scheme for the effective drainage of the growing town. He was at that time the leading authority on the subject: Chief Engineer to the Metropolitan Board of Works and responsible for building London's trunk and outfall sewers and the Thames Embankments. Bazalgette's system for Weston was swiftly implemented through two contracts: one for a 48 inch brick outfall sewer from the Drove Road works to the River Axe at Uphill; the other for an egg-shaped brick interceptor sewer from Orchard Street to the Drove Road site. This major scheme, involving 5000 yards of sewers in trenches that were sometimes at a depth of 25 feet, was completed in eighteen months and cost £17,000. The ground was difficult to work in, being soft and liable to slip. Frequent additions were made to Bazalgette's system over the remaining years of the century.

In other spheres limited companies stepped in to meet specific needs (often with some of the Commissioners as directors). It was a private company that built the first gasworks in Oxford Street in 1841 (opposite the end of New High Street, formerly known as

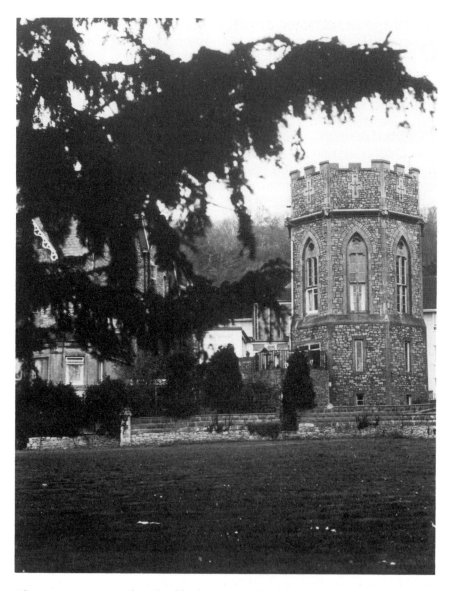

The water tower in the Shrubbery Estate, which had its own private water supply before the villas were connected to the waterworks company's system. The tower has been converted into a residence.

Gas Lane). As well as the 42 public lamps there were originally 50 private subscribers. The gasworks site was too central to be quite the thing in a fashionable resort, and new works were soon built 'out of town' at Drove Road (1852–6).

The same approach was adopted to the question of the water supply. Many houses, of course, had their own wells, and the large scale Ordnance Survey sheets of the 1880s show that there were also numerous communal wells in the poorer districts. Before tapped water was available more care was taken to avoid waste; in 1850 the public water pumps were padlocked because children had been wasting water. The Waterworks Company led by Henry Davies, was established in 1852 and built its reservoir on the site of natural springs in Milton road (at the bottom of Ashcombe Park), with a higher level tank in Lower Bristol Road by the gate lodge of Montpelier. The water was pumped up by steam engine. The quality of the water was said to be very pure but exceedingly hard. During one week in June 1891 the Ashcombe wells supplied over 3½ million gallons. The high level reservoir in Weston Woods was built in 1865, and the company was purchased by the Commissioners in 1878.

An unofficial volunteer fire brigade had been formed in 1846, at the behest of local traders. It was sponsored by the Commissioners and had a manual fire appliance. The Brigade was remodelled in 1879, and obtained a steam pump engine in the 1880s, when it had fourteen members who met for drill weekly.

Civic awareness and pride are in many respects the hallmarks of the Victorian age, and civic buildings the age's most apt symbol; for, if conditions were often dreadful and services inadequate in the new towns and cities, created in an era of *laissez-faire*, yet reforms and amelioration were equally the distinctive note as the century progressed. Society inevitably evolved new forms of organisation to cope with new realities. At Weston such enterprises were spread across a spectrum of different bodies, ranging from local government through commercial limited liability companies to philanthropic and charitable groups. The same names occur in different guises, and if this is interpreted as self-interest on the part of Weston's public men, then at least it was enlightened self-interest: they understood that the town's success, in which they had a stake, depended on the provision of more than the bare necessities. The public had high expectations. It was worth the community's while to provide, by one means or another, the refinements as

73

Christchurch, seen when construction was still under way, was built to serve the Montpelier Estate.

well as the basics. Within a generation the range of activity extended to include a whole host of new amenities and services.

The churches and chapels were behind many of the town's philanthropic endeavours. On the whole the Church of England predominated among the well-to-do. The building of new churches came early in the development of the new residential suburbs, although the first, Emmanuel Church in Oxford Street (1847) was a deliberately missionary undertaking directed at the working class population in that district. It had seating for 625 people. The first pastor was a remarkable man, the Revd John Hamilton Forsyth, who had been called 'the best B.A. in Cambridge', and who became curate at St John's in 1839 at the age of twenty-three. He worked tirelessly among the local poor, making friends and holding meetings in cottages and in the open air. He lived just long enough to see the new church opened before he died at the age of thirty-one. Christchurch (begun 1854) provided a focus for the new estate of Montpelier even before most of the villas there were built. In the same way Holy Trinity (1860) was the centrepiece of The Shrubbery and Cliftonville district, and was facetiously known as 'the hat shop' because of the display of wealth and fashion to be seen there every Sunday. All Saints (1898–1902), designed by G.F. Bodley in place of the temporary 'iron church', is one of the most impressive architecturally. St Paul's (1912) at the south end of Walliscote Road was heavily bombed during the Second World War.

A guidebook of 1850 declared: 'the Dissenting interest generally, in Weston, as in most watering places, is rather low, being greatly submerged by the attractive and more powerful influence of the Church'. Nevertheless the places of dissenting worship were more in evidence in the town centre, a telling sign of the resort's social geography. The first Methodist meetings were held in a converted cottage in Wellington Lane, but in 1847 a new Wesleyan Church opened in Regent Street and it was said that 'its Gothic architecture might easily be taken for an episcopal edifice.' In the 1860s this was enlarged to provide seating for 500. The building, on the corner of St James' Street, has been converted into a bank. It closed as a church in 1899. The Victoria Methodist Church in Station Road had opened in 1849 because the Regent Street church was too small; it was rebuilt in 1936 after a fire. There is another former Methodist Church to be seen on The Boulevard–Orchard Street corner. The United Methodists had a chapel in Burlington Street which was taken

The Congregational Church at the east end of Waterloo Street, built in 1876. The church was bombed during the Second World War, and the present building re-uses the Victorian foundations. The present church hall is on the site of the manse and school, to the left of the church.

over by the Bible Christians when the congregation moved to a site in Locking Road at the east end of The Plantation; this building later became a motor cycle shop.

An Independent Church was built in High Street in 1830, and before long this too was found to be inadequate. It was rebuilt in 1858. In 1876 the congregation moved to the Boulevard Congregational Church at the east end of Waterloo Street. The High Street building was purchased by Felix Thomas who converted it into an ironmonger's shop; the spire was taken down and incorporated in Banwell Abbey. The shop is now Woolworth's, and one can still see some of the buttresses and windows which betray its origins; the store was extended at the back, and the schoolroom and six cottages were demolished for the enlargement.

A third group to find rapid rebuilding necessary were the Baptists, who opened a church in Wadham Street in 1850. This building was enlarged in 1862 by Hans Price (his earliest known public commission). It is now being converted to the Blakehay, a new Arts and Community Centre. Price also designed the Baptist Church in Lower Bristol Road in 1870.

The Wadham Street Baptist Church of 1862–3, where Hans Price re-used the pillars and other details from the building of 1850. This is the earliest public building known to be by Price. *Woodspring Museum.*

The Bristol Road Baptist Church, 1870.

Land for a Friends' Meeting House had been given by Richard Parsley in Oxford Street in 1846 (another casualty of bomb damage). As with other Dissenting groups there is some evidence that wealthy Bristol merchants and others supported congregations at Weston. Not all the rich visitors to the resort were members of the established Church, and it was a prudent policy to help meet the needs of all. Roman Catholics were meeting at the Railway Hotel in 1853, and five years later they opened St Joseph's, tucked away on a small site on Pigott land in Camp Road. The cemetery was opened in 1856, well beyond the edge of town along the Bristol Road, with a gate lodge and gothic chapels, one of which survives. The old churchyard of St John's and the new churchyards at Emmanuel and Christchurch were closed for burials, and Holy Trinity, built soon afterwards, has no graveyard. The cemetery was extended in 1917, taking in the gate lodge of Ashcombe House, a detached mansion built by the Capells of Ashcombe, part of whose grounds formed the new extension.

It is evident that the combined congregations of all these churches added up to many hundreds in the later years of the century, their numbers regularly swollen by seasonal visitors.

All had their Sunday Schools and varied social activities, and all made a contribution to the town's welfare. Official provision for the relief of poverty was limited to the workhouse, which does not figure much in the town's annals; during its early years as a town Weston still formed part of the Axbridge Union and the workhouse was in the old market town. The Weston workhouse was built later on the edge of the hospital site by Baker Street. This was on glebe land belonging to Christchurch, which initiated many efforts to help poorer townspeople with 'outdoor relief'. There was a soup kitchen in Little Orchard Street, which in 1862 sold nearly 3000 quarts of soup to the poor at 1½d or 1d a pint. In 1866 a similar kitchen was opened in Carlton Street. At the north end of Alfred Street was the Christchurch Mission Room, now the Parish Hall.

A branch of the Church of England Temperance Society had been formed in the town and this gave the impetus for the opening of the British Workman, a cafe and temperance club, in 1876 in Meadow Street. In 1879 the Star Coffee House opened on the corner of Meadow Street and Alfred Street. It was originally a 'fourpenny dosshouse' offering cheap lodgings to vagrants, pedlars and poor workers. Later voluntary workers from Christchurch turned it into a cheap but respectable temperance hotel; a blazing fire was maintained winter and summer, its thick 'doorstep' sandwiches were well known, and it sold bottles of hot tea to men on their way to work in the early morning. The Star was in competition with the Alexandria public house on the opposite corner (renamed the Princess Alexandra), and the Bath Arms, a noted cider house, on the opposite corner of Alfred Street by the small open space.

A great proportion of the energies of Church and Chapel went into schooling for local children. At first this was the monopoly of the Church of England. The 1822 Guide mentions a school room for a hundred children which had recently opened. In 1835 Henry Law, the Rector, was active in founding what became the Emmanuel Infants School, which was run on voluntary subscription until 1894. Ten years later the National School was opened at the bottom of Lower Church Road (now part of the College site); pupils paid 2d a week, or 1d if more than one child from a family attended. An appeal for contributions was made to visitors because their presence during the summer months 'created a demand for juvenile labour to attend donkeys'; in the winter they relied on the charity of residents and these boys 'thrown adrift on the world should have the advantage of a sound religious education'.

Dissenters were becoming active in education during the 1840s. A Mechanics Institute, for adults, opened in 1846 under the presidency of the Revd Mr Hopkins, minister of the Independent Church. After a false start in 1851, the British School (under the auspices of the British and Foreign Schools Society) was built in Hopkins Street in 1855. John Palmer the builder donated the land, and most of the original committee were local tradesmen: Joseph James, another builder, James Harvey, bathing machine proprietor, Joseph Sturge, ironmonger, Henry Pond, brightsmith, John Rossiter, watchmaker, Henry Langdon, licensed victualler. The building, 'Elizabethan in character', still stands with a later extension. Funds remained a problem, and the fees of 6d a week were high compared to the National School's. Nevertheless there were 137 children on the books by 1858, with 90 in average attendance.

The Church of England's influence remained predominant. In 1859 Miss Salter, sharing the perennial concern about the donkey boys, set up a night school in a room in Carlton Street, assisted by Mr Mable, a cobbler, and this developed into the Albert Memorial School (1863) next to Emmanuel Church; the building was demolished to make way for the Town Hall extension. In the same year the Christchurch Elementary School opened.

Rivalry between the religious parties was intensified after Forster's Education Act of 1870, which pointed towards the principle of compulsory education for all children, to be secured if necessary by the establishment of local School Boards. Mr A. Hutson has charted in detail the complex manoeuvres of the Church of England in Weston which successfully delayed the establishment of a Board for twenty-three years. Fear of a rise in the rates played a part, together with desire for control of religious teaching. The Anglicans controlled three-quarters of Weston's school places, and moved swiftly to provide more, following a notice from the Education Department which found the total insufficient: a new building next to the Christchurch School opened in 1874, the 'United Infants'. The cases for and against a School Board were eagerly canvassed in the local press.

The most remarkable element in the Anglican tactics was positive action to keep the British School open. The British School was in financial difficulties in the mid-seventies, but if it

The Board School in Walliscote Road, built in 1897 'on the Prussian model'.

had closed the loss of school places in the town would have made it impossible to keep the spectre of a Board at bay. A relatively modest outlay averted this threat. Extensions were built to the National School in 1879, and to Christchurch, to keep pace with the growing population, but finally the financial strain of keeping up this race against numbers was too much. A School Board was finally established in 1893, and took control of some of the existing schools.

It took four years to build the first Board School, in Walliscote Road. Hans Price designed the splendid building, which has been described as one of the finest Board Schools in England. The second Board School was built in Locking Road (close to the unfinished St. Saviour's) in 1900. In 1903 control of local education passed to Somerset County Council.

Hans Price also designed the School of Science and Art in Lower Church Road, the first proper higher education establishment, with large studio windows on the north side, although classes had been undertaken for some years previously. In 1900 the Museum and Public Library opened in The Boulevard; a museum collection had been kept in the Albert Memorial Hall for some time. The new building was partly paid for by public subscription and partly by a bequest of Mr Frederick Wood of

The School of Science and Art in Lower Church Road. On the north side are large studio windows, and the façade incorporates decorative ceramic tiles.

Chew Magna, who also donated his reference library, valued at £4000, and promised to leave a legacy of £1000 to the town if a suitable building was erected. The building was extended in 1932, and is still the main public library (now Woodspring Central Library).

Side by side with the schools for local children there were numerous private schools for the children of the better off which flourished in the resort's healthy climate. Many were quite small, occupying villas built as private dwellings. Among the larger schools were Eastern House in Landemann Circus, and The College, purpose built in Beach Road by Jonathon Elwell (subsequently converted into the Grand Atlantic Hotel after enlargements). F.A. Knight, whose books on the Mendip Country remain classics, was a teacher at Brynmelyn in Landemann Circus. Weston attracted private schools not only because of its

The Public Library in The Boulevard (now Woodspring Central Library). The façade has statues by Harry Hems.

The College, Beach Road, before it was enlarged as the Grand Atlantic Hotel; one of many private schools in Victorian Weston.

The original hospital, built on part of the glebe land of Christchurch in the 1860s and approached from the northern section of Alfred Street. There were subsequently many additions to this original bulding.

climate, but because it was respectable and genteel. Parents who were abroad in the colonies could entrust their children to such institutions. There were at least thirty private schools in Weston before the First World War, and their disappearance began only after the Second.

Medical provision was limited to private doctors and a dispensary until the 1860s, when a subscription was opened for the building of a hospital. The move followed a serious accident to a building workman. Hans Price designed the original building on glebe land in Alfred Street. Other wards were added in the following decades, and in the 1920s a fresh campaign led by Henry Butt resulted in the new General Hospital, adjoining the original but facing The Boulevard. Price had also designed part of the Royal West of England Hospital, known as the Sanatorium, at the south end of the Esplanade, which opened in 1868.

Hans Price gave to the town a collection of public buildings displaying individuality of style and civic dignity. With such commissions he was free from the constraints of domestic

The Royal West of England Hospital, at the southern end of the Beach Lawns, seen from its grounds that stretched to the sand dunes.

architecture and could give fuller expression to his interest in blending and experimenting with elements from different styles. Public buildings perhaps typify the Victorian period more than any other, but at a time when architecture always ran the risk of being debased through a preoccupation with gimmickry and detail, Price showed that ornament, however profuse, could still be used to create an overall effect and blend with earlier buildings. Most of Price's public buildings are now listed. To those already mentioned should be added others which are also 'public' in character, such as the St Kew Masonic Lodge in The Boulevard (now the Constitutional Club), which has lost the wooden turret that was formerly such an idiosyncratic contribution to the skyline. On the opposite corner, close to the St. John's Church Hall, is the building Price designed for the *Weston Mercury* in 1885. It is still used by the paper, which absorbed its rival, the *Weston Gazette* in the 1950s. Moreover the paper

The offices of the *Weston Mercury* in Waterloo Street; designed by Hans Price in 1885 and still occupied by the local newspaper.

remains independent and owned by the family which has run it since James Dare started it as *The Westonian* in 1843. It has reflected all the controversies and news generated by local life, and forms a unique record of the community.

The most obvious of Price's public buildings is the Town Hall. Weston's Commissioners had met at first in borrowed premises but chose the site for a town hall in the 1850s. Controversy soon erupted, however, because the land was on the northern fringe of Richard Parsley's old Whitecross Estate, which had been acquired by Joseph Whereat and Henry Davies. As Davies was the Clerk to the Commissioners it was felt that this was a move to enhance his new investment. Work began in 1858, but the dispute was not settled until the Rector, Archdeacon Law, bought the new building and made a free gift of it to the town in the following year. This building is now the Assembly Room, and its round-headed windows, typical of the period, can be seen from the small yard adjoining the churchyard of Emmanuel. It is now incorporated into the larger complex, constructed in 1897 to a design by Price, who remodelled the 'Big Ben' clock tower and added the entrance loggia and southern wing; a further addition of 1927 masks the original building beneath the tower. These elements achieve a confident unity and presence, immediately conveying function and purpose: this is how a public building ought to look, whatever the particular style. The Commissioners, who had previously taken on the functions of a Board of Health, had given way to an Urban District Council in 1894.

The town's public buildings mark half a century of expansion, confidence and achievement, at a time when the nation's optimism and wealth found unique expression in the seaside. As well as the buildings, the spaces between them tell the same story, for parks and gardens are part of the fabric of the town, created to cater for residents and visitors who expected quality in their surroundings. As we have seen, there is no one central or predominant public open space. The first wave of landscaped gardens was created in the residential suburbs: The Shrubbery, Eastfield Gardens, Park Place, Ellenborough Park. In the later years of consolidation that followed housing-led development, public parks appeared on the scene. Flagstaff Hill was turned into the Prince Consort Gardens soon after the opening of Birnbeck Pier in 1867, which brought new activity to this end of the hillside. In 1883 the town acquired the site of Clarence Park through the generosity of Rebecca Davies, widow of Henry.

The original Town Hall of 1858, and behind it Emmanuel Church in Oxford Street. In 1897 Price extended and remodelled the Town Hall for the new Urban District Council, adapting the campanile as a clock tower. The northern block immediately below the tower was added in 1927.

Prince Consort Gardens being laid out. Wattle fences were used to protect trees and shrubs from the sand and salt of the prevailing westerly winds blowing off the sea. It required great labour to establish gardens in parts of the town close to the shore.

Following the opening of the new railway station, Old Station Square eventually became The Plantation, rechristened Alexandra Gardens (1909). The Recreation Grounds were opened on the other side of the new station in 1885 to cater for the new interest in sports, which could also be indulged in the new parks themselves. Ashcombe Park was laid out with grand avenues, the site having been safeguarded some years before.

In 1889 the Smyth Pigott family decided to leave The Grove, and it was at first proposed to sell the site for building; such was the public outcry that the grounds were acquired by the town for a yearly rent charge of £300 and Grove Park as we know it was created, with the bandstand and shelters that were soon provided. This seems to symbolise the shift from manorial to municipal power which had been taking place throughout the previous half century; in the 1890s the public crowded into what had once been the squire's exclusive preserve, and the great era of open air concerts began. By this time the grandest of all the open spaces in the resort had been laid out, the Beach Lawns, part of an ambitious sea front improvement scheme. Thus within a decade the town had acquired very significant additions to its green open spaces and further enhanced the quality of life and leisure both for visitors and residents.

WHAT TO SEE

• Early shopping streets: St James' Street; Meadow Street (west end).

• Commercial buildings: central and north High Street; Waterloo Street; Magdala Buildings (opposite The Odeon); National Westminster Bank, South Parade.

• Churches: Emmanuel, Oxford Street; Christchurch, Montpelier; Holy Trinity, Atlantic Road; All Saints, All Saints Road. Cemetery, Lower Bristol Road. St Joseph's (Roman Catholic), Camp Road.

• Chapels: Primitive Methodist, Burlington Street; Baptist Church, Wadham Street; Baptist Church, Lower Bristol Road; Boulevard United Reformed Church, Waterloo Street.

• Schools: British School, Hopkins Street; Christchurch, Baker Street; Board School, Walliscote Road; Eastern House, Landemann Circus.

• Public buildings by Hans Price: Library, The Boulevard; School of Science and Art, Lower Church Road; Constitutional Club, The Boulevard; Mercury offices, Waterloo Street; Town Hall.

• Parks: Grove Park; Prince Consort Gardens (above Birnbeck); Clarence Park, Walliscote Road; Ashcombe Park, Milton Road.

Sea Front Schemes

Weston Bay, which was the reason for the town's existence, inspired numerous schemes of improvement and exploitation throughout the nineteenth century, some of which were actually implemented. The coastline at Weston is composed of a conjunction of elements unusual in this part of the country: the dramatic sweep of the bay, the headlands formed by the tip of the Mendips, and the fine distant views. Early visitors were content to enjoy the scenery for its own sake and profit from the healthy atmosphere. Amusements were simple – donkeys or ponies to ride, sea bathing, and boat trips. The first esplanade of 1826 ended opposite the Assembly Rooms at Regent Street, although it was later extended as far as Carlton Street. Knightstone and Anchor Head were the landing places for boats, with slipways from the 1820s, when steamers were established in the Bristol Channel and a range of local boats was available for pleasure trips.

Landing was a problem at Weston, because of the distance the tide recedes, and this was a difficulty at other resorts which were not old ports. Often smaller craft were used for embarking or landing, and sometimes visitors were even carried on the backs of porters. Piers were developed initially to solve this problem. Ryde Pier (1813–14) which extended 1250 feet into the sea was a great success because of the new steamers, and other soon followed. At Weston Knightstone became a kind of pier after its causeway was built up, but even so the hours during which boats could land here were limited.

Steamers used both Anchor Head and the Axe Estuary as traffic increased during the 1840s with the town's expansion. The first steamer to run an excursion from Weston was the *Sampson*, a tug, chartered by Captain Stone in 1843. She was a big tug for her day, and attended the launching of Brunel's Atlantic liner the *SS Great Britain*. Old paddle tugs were often more generously built than later ones, and were fitted with

91

additional platforms and awnings when used for pleasure trips.

In September 1845 Captain Coles chartered the *Air* to take 140 passengers from Weston to Newport, and in the following year chartered her for the first Weston to Minehead excursion. Such trips were special occasions in the days before regular services became established, highlights of the local season, as this description of an excursion from Brown's *Weekly Advertiser* of 1847 illustrates:

> The beach was lined with spectators. The vessel is the *Air*. She is a very fine boat and admirably fitted up for passengers. She sailed about nine o'clock, having on board about 150 highly respectable visitors and residents. The whole of the Swiss band was in attendance, and the fineness of the weather and the beautiful scenery of the Channel, and ever and anon the peals of music swelling on the breeze, must have rendered the excursion extremely delightful for those on board. The party returned to Weston about 9 p.m.

The success of the Channel steamers helped to fuel speculation about the wider commercial possibilities. While Brunel's Bristol and Exeter Railway was still under construction in 1841 the Bristol General Steam Navigation Company had begun building an iron steam vessel, the *Taff*, for 'the station between Uphill and Cardiff'. The following year the press carried advertisements for the project to 'unite the Taff and Exeter Railways'. 'The establishment of a general carrying trade throughout the Channel affords almost certain success to the undertaking', said the notice, adding that every possible encouragement short of a monopoly would be given to anyone who would establish a regular service. Nevertheless the scheme fell through, although it was the forerunner of several similar projects.

In 1845 the Weston-super-Mare Packet Station, Landing Pier and Slip Company was formed with £40,000 capital raised through £50 shares. John Hugh Smyth Pigott was chairman, with twenty shares, and offered to give the necessary land and approach roads and whatever stone and wood were required. Other prominent Weston figures involved included Richard Parsley, William Cox Junior, Francis Hutchinson Synge and Joseph Whereat. The engineer was James Dredge of Bath, whose plans were approved by a public meeting held in the Temperance Hall. Sketches originally issued by the company had shown a stone

James Dredge's proposed chain pier would have been a suspension bridge linking Birnbeck Island and the mainland, and would have been only the second chain pier in the country.

jetty south of Birnbeck Island, but Dredge proposed a chain pier or suspension bridge between the island and the mainland, with a span of 545 feet. Work had started on Brunel's great suspension bridge at Clifton in 1840, and Dredge himself had unsuccessfully entered designs for this project. There was only one chain pier in the country, at Brighton (1822–3). Suspension chains hung from cables between massive towers, and the deck hung from the chains, the ends of which were anchored at each end beyond the towers. The fact that there was an island at Birnbeck, where the seaward end could be anchored, made this an attractive solution for Weston. In general chain piers did not catch on; at Brighton the deck was always liable to wind damage, and the whole pier was destroyed in the 1890s. The only other chain pier ever built in this country was at Sea View on the Isle of Wight (1880), which was more successful and lasted until 1950.

The Birnbeck chain pier was defeated by the sheer force of the currents. The first of the great stone pillars was washed away by the tide, although some of the foundations can still be made out at low water on the north side of the present pier. Work was restarted, and in April 1847 Dredge undertook to finish the work in twelve months at a cost of £10,000, to be paid in instalments.

August 1848 saw the company taking legal action to recover its money from the engineer. The work was far from finished, and, having been again abandoned, was now useless. The company was awarded damages of £1400. A local poet supplied the epitaph for the ill-fated project:

> Alas for the Pier! that wonderful Pier!
> 'Twas to bring Westonians some thousands a-year;
> Ships, schooners, and brigs all in multitudes here
> Were to come from Japan, and South Wales, and Cape Clear;
> And steamers by dozens were soon to appear.

Another ambitious scheme was launched a few years later, this time for the Uphill end of the bay. In 1854 the Weston-super-Mare Pier, Steam Ferry and Railway Company raised £20,000 in £10 shares, proposing to lay a railway line three-quarters of a mile long from the main line to a pier at Uphill, where the port would be equipped with warehouses and hydraulic cranes. Francis Hutchinson Synge (who lived at Weston Lodge at the bottom of Lower Bristol Road) was again prominent in the venture. It is surprising that a scheme of this kind was contemplated for the south end of the bay where the narrow creek at Uphill was a check on the expansion of trade with larger vessels. Equally surprising to us is the persistence of local speculators in backing schemes of this kind, but we should remember that this was an era of unparalleled industrial expansion; it was the high noon of Victorianism, and the growth rate exceeded any that had previously been known, or that has been known since. Development projects were in the air everywhere.

The next bout of optimism reverted to the north end of the bay. By this time Weston's Lord of the Manor was the irascible John Hugh Wadham Pigott Smyth Pigott, an enthusiastic patron of the Weston Regatta who suffered great humiliation because of the resort's inadequate landing facilities. During the regatta of 1856 the winds were such that, after the event, five of the gentlemen taking part were unable to land in order to attend the public dinner marking the occasion. Worse still, the winner of the cup was prevented from landing and was thus unable to receive the company's congratulations. A journalist reporting the event in *Bell's Life* stressed the need for a pier or landing slip, but doubted whether one would ever be built, adding that 'every man in this delightful town, being jealous of everybody else, in the true dog and manger spirit, he won't do anything himself for the good of the place, and he won't let anybody else'. This was a little unfair, especially as the Anchor Head landing slip was actually improved in 1856, but it did underline the difficulty. In 1859 Pigott and his associates produced another plan, for a solid masonry embankment curving southward from the mainland towards the southern tip of Birnbeck. 'It will turn the current which now flows so rapidly at every ebb and flood in its confined space, and render the actual basin a perfectly safe and well sheltered harbour, sufficiently capacious to hold a fleet of from fifty to sixty sail.' A railway would run from just above the new jetty to the main line at Puxton, and there would be a lighthouse on the island. Optimistic predictions were made about the effects of the altered currents on the sand and mud in the bay. The scheme would result in Weston and the neighbourhood 'becoming a great entrepôt of mineral and other traffic'. Like its predecessors the project came to nothing.

Attention again veered to the south of the bay, but this time the speculators had learnt the lesson that they needed deep water. Uphill was abandoned in favour of the headland of Brean Down across the Axe Estuary. The Brean Down Harbour Company was incorporated in 1861 with capital of £350,000. The chairman was Sir John Eardley Wilmot of Swiss Villa. Again the idea hinged on prospects of commercial traffic between South Wales

The proposal for Brean Down Harbour: a sketch based on drawings issued when the scheme was begun in 1864. The view is taken from the Brean Down Fort, which was built nearby on the tip of the headland.

and the West of England: agricultural produce from the West Country would be exchanged for coal from South Wales. Experts testified before a House of Commons Select Committee to the immense scope for such trade. It was planned to build a breakwater at the end of Brean Down on the north side, and to connect the docks there with the main line by a railway running along the headland. The landing slip was to be 11,000 feet long and 35 feet broad, and there would be three divisons of docks giving a total wharfage of one and a half miles.

Work began at about the same time as construction of a nearby military installation, the Brean Down Fort, on the very tip of the Down. Palmerston's government had responded to scares about a possible French invasion, and French innovations with iron-clad battleships, by commissioning a string of new coastal defences, including four sites which between them would command the Bristol Channel approaches to Bristol and Cardiff: Lavernock in Wales, Steep Holm, Flat Holm and Brean Down. The present 'military road' along the Down was built to serve the fort, which remained in use until it was partially destroyed by an explosion in 1900. During the 1860s, therefore, this quiet promontory south of Weston saw unprecedented building activity. Lady Eardley Wilmot had laid the foundation stone for the harbour on 5th November 1864, in front of a party of celebrities and the town band who had crossed in a paddle steamer, the *Wye*. Unfortunately the stone was too light, and next morning both the stone and its marker buoy were found to have floated out to Steep Holm. Despite this inauspicious beginning work continued until a violent storm in December 1872 destroyed the jetty. The scheme was revived in 1887, but sufficient capital could not be raised. This was the most spectacular of the disasters that attended the many projects for Weston Bay.

'It would appear almost incredible that a watering place so matured in its pretensions, so conveniently situated, and so well frequented as Weston-super-Mare, should to this day be without a pier.' So began the prospectus, issued in 1864, of the company that was to succeed where others had failed and secure the building of Birnbeck Pier. It was probably a blessing in disguise that Weston had had to wait for its pier so long. In the event the town secured the services of the most famous pier builder of the age, Eugenius Birch, and obtained a structure which used the latest technology, capable of overcoming the difficulties posed by the strong currents.

Birnbeck Pier, built to Eugenius Birch's designs (1864–1867). The site at the end of Worlebury Hill afforded a deep water anchorage at all tides. *Andrew Eddy.*

Early piers had been functional. Companies had sold shares on the expected return from tolls on goods and passengers. As the Victorian seaside approached its zenith, however, a growing public was discovering the leisure potential of such structures: a place to stroll and take exercise, where the thrill of being at sea could be experienced without the inconvenience of actually leaving dry land. Birch's design reflects this new view of 'pleasure piers', built with the enjoyment of promenaders in mind as well as the needs of passengers and traders. The General Pier and Harbour Act of 1861 made the business of promoting a pier scheme much easier; after this date proposals for building piers and collecting tolls usually received assent. Notwithstanding the astonished tones of the Weston company's prospectus, Birnbeck got its pier early in the two decades that saw the golden age of British pier building.

The Lord of the Manor was again a director of the new company, but this time his highly competent agent, Robert Landemann Jones, was the chairman. Mr Baker the solicitor was secretary. The new management team was in charge. Two thousand shares were offered at £10 each. The components of the pier were prefabricated to Birch's design by Richard and John Laybourne at their Isca Foundry at Newport. By this time Birch (1818–1884) was pre-eminent in the field. He had gained experience as a railway engineer in this country and in India, and indeed his career illustrates how the technology of Victorian industrialism could produce 'spin-offs' for the leisure market which developed during the century as its mirror image. While building Margate Jetty in 1853 Birch had pioneered the use of screw piles for driving the uprights into the sea bed. He was to design fourteen seaside piers altogether, including Blackpool North, Brighton West, Aberystwyth and Eastbourne. It was his

Details of Birnbeck Pier's ironwork. Birch used the cast iron components in a design that achieved great rigidity by calculating the forces of tension and compression. *Andrew Eddy*.

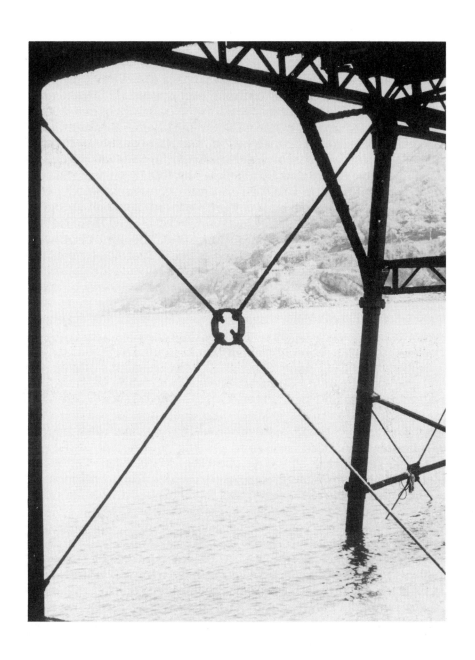

achievement to develop the promenade pier proper. Earlier piers had been largely bare and devoid of interest above deck. At Brighton Birch took his inspiration from the Royal Pavilion (and perhaps from his memories of India) and created the ornate and vaguely Oriental architecture which is the hallmark of the classic pier and of so many other seaside buildings. Brighton and Birnbeck were under construction simultaneously and have important similarities, but whereas Brighton Pier has received substantial later additions Birnbeck is much as Birch designed it.

Piers exploited Britain's lead in civil engineering during the Victorian era. The solid masonry jetty was replaced by an open lattice-like structure, which was cheaper and offered little resistance to the tide; it also made moorings safer. The use of iron was the breakthrough. Timber in the sea is liable to attack by marine worm in a surprisingly short time. Cast iron became *the* material, strong in compression and very resistant to corrosion if of good quality. The iron columns were cast circular, making them less resistant to currents than square ones. At Birnbeck the columns are in fifteen clusters of four, morticed into the rock to a depth of three or four feet. The columns in each group are linked by tie rods twisted round each other in the centre of the tower, an unusual arrangement. From an engineering point of view the system of struts and ties is considered to be especially interesting; this provides rigidity, harnessing the forces of tension and compression. For these joists wrought iron was the ideal material, lighter than cast iron and having a different torsional strength. The deck is of wood, allowing for drainage. The main pier is 1040 feet long and over 20 feet wide. The northern arm, the actual steamer jetty, continued to incorporate wooden piles to absorb the shock from boats docking.

The approaches were blasted through solid rock. The stone toll house at the entrance originally had a conspicuous bell turret to announce sailings. At the laying of the foundation stone an awkward question of precedence arose between the notoriously aristocratically-minded Lord of the Manor and the 'upstart' Commissioners. This was solved by having the ceremony performed by the squire's young son, Master Cecil Smyth Pigott, and he also officially opened the pier on 5th June 1867. The day was a general holiday. As well as the official dinner in the Town Hall, another dinner was held at which six hundred ·people sat down to eat in the Market Hall. Admission to the pier originally cost one penny, but the price was doubled at the end of the first

Detail of the Isca Foundry's ironwork in the canopy of Birnbeck's main pavilion.

season after 120,000 people had been admitted in three months. The first paddle steamer, the *Heather Belle* from Cardiff, had called on the first day of opening.

Although there was great rejoicing at the pier's opening, it soon became obvious that the venture was not going to prove a rapid commercial success. The rail connection envisaged in the early plans had not materialised. Birnbeck relied very heavily on the leisure market. Maintenance costs were high and profits low. The pavilion and reading room were not completed until 1884, but the unique feature of Birnbeck Pier – its island – meant that these could be real buildings in stone. Also in 1884 the 'made ground' on the island was asphalted, and a tramway was built to carry luggage from the steamers. Three years later a switchback was in use, one of numerous 'fairground' amusements that crowded the island in the late Victorian and Edwardian heyday.

In 1893 Campbells chartered an old iron paddle steamer, the *Sea Breeze*, to establish themselves on the Weston-Cardiff run, and there was a period of spirited competition between

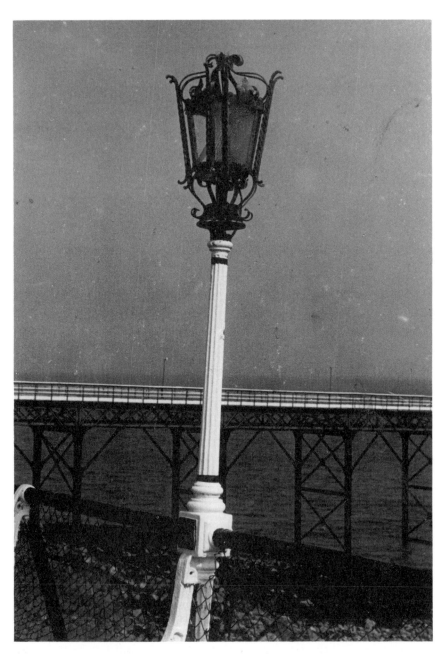

One of the original gas lamps along the main structure of Birnbeck Pier. The gas supply was carried inside the rail at the back of the continuous seating.

102

A steamer approaching the jetty at Birnbeck. This form of transport was second only to the railway in importance at Weston in the resort's heyday.

Campbells and Edwards and Robinson of Cardiff. On one occasion two boats, the *Ravenwood* and the *Lorna Doone*, collided while racing for the jetty. It was common for rival boats to try to beat each other to landing points around the coast in order to attract the bulk of the waiting passengers. Gradually Campbells, with their experience of operating on the Clyde, gained the upper hand. Their White Funnel fleet – the 'swans' – dominated the Channel steamer trade in the later years. A lifeboat station had opened on the north side of the pier in 1881, the boat being slung from davits until a boat house was built in 1889. The second boat-house was built on the south side, for easier launching, in 1902, and this is still functional. It has the longest slipway of any lifeboat station in the country. Over the years the local volunteer crew has saved many lives, and is a part of the local story which compels both gratitude and pride.

In 1892 a new low water steamer jetty opened to the south of the island, to cope with the increased volume of traffic. There were sometimes half a dozen vessels waiting to unload. It was estimated that an average August Bank Holiday might bring boats landing fifteen thousand people. In 1898 a new jetty was opened on the south west, 125 feet long, and this was used until

The second lifeboat station on the south side of the island at Birnbeck. The clock tower in the background was an important feature in the days of a busy steamer timetable.

it was destroyed in the great gale of 1903. Its replacement was in use from 1910 to 1916. The north jetty was also rebuilt after the gale, this time in steel, and was extended to 300 feet.

By the end of the century Birnbeck Pier was clearly prosperous. More and more people were able to take holidays, and travelling to the seaside was cheaper. Vast numbers of Welsh miners came to Birnbeck on steamer trips; many, on landing, got no farther, never entering the town at all but remaining on the island. The bar was one attraction, and others included tea and coffee rooms, a band, photographic studios, bazaars selling souvenirs, shooting galleries, swings, and (rare in those days) a telephone. The pier company had its own bye-laws to control behaviour. In 1894 there were thirty-five bye-laws, eighteen of which carried penalties ranging from £2 to £5. Visitors were forbidden to 'halloo, shout or call out, or blow, strike or sound any gong, or other instrument, or make any other noise beyond that of ordinary speaking'. On Boxing Day, 1897, fire destroyed the main buildings including the concert hall, pavilion and refreshment rooms. It is a sign of the company's healthy state at this time that, at 9 o'clock next morning, Hans Price's practice was instructed to draw up plans for rebuilding. The new buildings opened in July 1898. They incorporate columns from the Isca Foundry and are impressive in their own right, worthy of the pier and worthy of Price.

Birnbeck's eventual prosperity, after its faltering start, reflected the fortunes of the resort as a whole. The same determination to fight back against recession and to adjust to new markets produced the most impressive monument of all, and one so extensive, indeed, that it can almost be taken for granted. This is the sea front itself, or rather the Sea Front Improvement Scheme which created the present appearance of the resort's waterfront. The earliest part of the scheme to be proposed was the levelling of the 'tots' or sand dunes and their replacement by gardens; an undertaking that something of this sort would be done had been given earlier in the century to the owners of the Whitecross Estate, where Ellenborough Crescent and other properties were being built. The dunes caused great problems because of drifting sand. However the scheme as it actually took shape was first mooted by Edwin Knight, chairman of the local Board of Commissioners, at a private dinner. In December 1879 the board appointed a committee to undertake the negotiations. There was lobbying for rival schemes which included the acquisition of Grove Park and the creation of a public garden at the Hotel Field or Rogers' Field (which later became the Winter Gardens).

The resort was at a crossroads. There were many empty houses. The nationwide recession of the 1870s had left many unemployed, especially in the building trades which had enjoyed boom years at Weston during the resort's earlier period of rapid growth. Some of the upper classes were abandoning Weston in favour of more remote watering places such as Torquay, where the railways and the excursionist had not yet penetrated. Weston was attracting more and more people, but of a lower class; if they were to be accommodated, more space had to be opened up. Was the town to act positively to cater for the new market or was it to rest on its laurels? Mr Knight offered the Sea Front Improvement Scheme as a 'boon to the working classes' and one which could be carried through more cheaply during a recession than at any other time.

SKETCH OF OPEN KIOSK

SKETCH OF KIOSK

SKETCH OF LADIES' CLOAK ROOM

Details from the sketch plans for the Sea Front Improvement Scheme prepared by Mr T.J. Scoones.

106

The Board had to secure government sanction for the borrowing of £28,000, and before this was obtained the whole idea had stirred up violent local controversy.

> During the whole course of these difficult negotiations there was great opposition to the whole scheme, and some extraordinary antagonistic plans were exhibited. Absurd rumours were freely circulated; persons who were in favour of the scheme being carried out were frequently met with derision; a Ratepayers' Protection Association was established, and every effort was made to effect the abandonment of the project. But an election of Commissioners taking place, all the candidates favourable to carrying out the work were returned . . .

Five hundred people attended an excited public meeting in the Town Hall on 27th April 1881. It was said that the scheme was not what was needed; that it was too expensive; that there had been too much secrecy; that the wall would be washed away; that there should be a choice of plans. Much of the criticism focused on the creation of 'artificial' flower gardens, with fountains, trees, shrubs, cascades and kiosks. It was said that the plants would be blighted by sea winds in such an exposed situation, and that the cost of upkeep and constant replacement would be colossal; it would be better to create 'a greensward for cricket and football exercises'. A resolution opposing the scheme was overwhelmingly carried.

The official enquiry was held in February 1882. For the Ratepayers' Association Captain Battiscombe argued that visitors preferred the open sand and dunes for walking. 'Take away the freedom and freshness of those, and you spoil the natural beauty and pleasant area of the shore.' Colonel Turner, J.P., said that the local magistrates had found the advent of excursionists very undesirable. He thought the scheme would only draw more excursionists, and not the class of visitor it was desired to attract to the town. At one level the debate reflected a tension which is perennial at Weston, as at other seaside towns, between residents wishing to 'pull up the drawbridge', maintain the status quo, and avoid higher rates, and those seeking new developments to attract or retain more visitors. At a deeper level the issue crystallised choices facing the resort at a critical moment, and revealed the importance of social and class feeling. Much of the opposition was opposition to social change rather than to

Early occupants of one of the original shelters.

environmental damage. It is significant that previous commercial projects seem to have aroused practically no strong passions, although the implications of some of them would appear to have been equally devastating, if not more so.

The result of the enquiry was that a reduced loan was sanctioned subject to the plans for the gardens being dropped. On 15th March 1883 the Lord of the Manor, Cecil Smyth Pigott, laid the foundation stone in Glentworth Bay. Altogether the work was to require 175,000 tons of ballast, stone and material; 85,000 cubic yards of earthwork infilling; 20,000 cubic yards of masonry; 9000 yards of metalling; 49,000 yards of asphalting; and 4000 yards of iron runner fencing. The engineer was Mr T.J. Scoones of Bristol, who was already working in the area for the Great Western Railway. The contractor was Mr Krauss of Bristol. The project was one of the biggest civil engineering undertakings of its kind in the region, and all the work had to be carried out between tides. It was considered a great feat that the whole of the foundations (on terrain varying from rock to clay and quicksand) were got in without the use of coffer dams. The work was always vulnerable, and there was one major setback, a bad gale on 17th

The sweep of Weston Bay made the improvement scheme an impressive achievement. The wide promenade and simple stone wall blend to enhance dramatic vistas.

109

October 1883 which destroyed about a quarter of a mile of the wall: debris was strewn down Regent Street and West Street. Yet the main scheme was completed in under three years.

There were three main elements: the replacement of the sand dunes by lawns; a carriage road; and, by the sea wall itself, an esplanade. The last two were carried out 'into the sea' over the beach by as much as forty feet in some places, and this explains the drop down to the sands from the promenade. The work stretched from the Royal West of England Hospital to Glentworth Bay, and was almost immediately extended northward to Birnbeck Pier; a length of some two and half miles. It secured the whole of the sea front for public use, an apparently obvious objective but one not always met at other resorts. The fact that all the elements were carried through as a complete scheme, on the grand scale, is what makes it so impressive a monument. The Commissioners had come a long way in forty years. It is well known that the tide rise here is the second highest in the world. To devise a scheme that could withstand the Atlantic gales, look stylish, and create space for thousands of visitors was a major

Looking south from Knightstone Causeway. The iron fencing was felt to be a necessary safety measure to protect pedestrians from road traffic. Most of the fencing was removed in the 1960s.

The improvement scheme was extended north of Knightstone, circling Glentworth Bay or the 'Little Sands'.

achievement, especially in an age when work was still done by hand without the benefit of modern machinery. On 4th December 1885 *Building News* reported:

> There are numerous points of interest in the plans, but we can only briefly enumerate such conveniences as frequent breaks in the wall, giving shelter niches with seats, many steps and accesses to sands and beach, together with eight têtes-du-point thrown out from the line of the wall, and forming promenades with side entrances to sands. In the centre of these are placed shelter kiosks, two of them closed and used as cloak rooms and lavatories. The sheltered seats in kiosks and niches will accommodate over 500 people, and the lounge seats on the Esplanade about 900 people.

The most important visual quality is the overall simplicity of design, which was emphasised by the substitution of lawns for intricate formal gardens. The scheme is bold and dramatic, taking its cue from the curve of the bay, which it civilises without cluttering unduly. The parapet wall is of stone, and, since Weston is a stone town (one of the very few resorts to enjoy

At Anchor Head and Birnbeck the walls reach an impressive height, and this end of the sea front has a distinctive character which complements the main length of the scheme.

a good local supply), this relates the sea front to the town behind, enforcing its distinctive character. At the northern end the wall rises with the hill like part of a medieval castle, giving a comforting impression of strength.

One can understand why some local ratepayers had found the economics of the proposals daunting. The cost (less than £30,000) would be millions today. At the time Weston's population was only just over 13,000. The town's rateable value was not much more than £60,000. The project was a huge gamble financially, but it paid off. Whereas it had been proposed to put between 2d. and 5d. in the pound onto the rates for three or four years, it was found that the immediate increase in rateable value and the generally increased prosperity enabled the work to be completed without increasing the rates. The whole scheme is an interesting example of a local authority spending its way out of a recession long before Keynesian principles were formulated.

The whole length of the work carried out under the scheme is substantially unchanged and can still be appreciated today. Indeed, some sections around the Marine Lake or Glentworth

Bay have recently been restored after having been hidden by a concrete extension for many years during this century. The 1880s saw Weston turn definitely into a more popular resort with a wider appeal. It was the leisure-oriented projects that were successful rather than those inspired by industrial trade and commerce. With its new railway loop and station, the delayed developments at Birnbeck at last completed, and the sea front scheme, the town had become what we still see today, and the stage was set for the late Victorian and Edwardian heyday of the resort.

WHAT TO SEE

• Brean Down Fort, on the western tip of the headland (approach the Down from Brean village).

• Birnbeck Pier, tollhouse, pavilion, steamer jetty, lifeboat station.

• Sea wall, esplanade, and carriage road from Glentworth Bay (Marine Lake) to the Royal West of England Hospital; Beach Lawns south from the Grand Pier.

Work and Play

The eventual prosperity of Birnbeck Pier and the successful completion of the Sea Front Improvement Scheme marked Weston's change into a 'popular' resort. It was by now catering for crowds rather than individuals, and the nature of the seaside experience which it offered changed as more people were able to come here to enjoy it. The resort had received occasional crowds of visitors since the first excursion trains began coming in the 1840s. In the next decade they became more common. The Bristol and Exeter Railway began organising its own excursion trains, and more and more parties from inland towns and cities began discovering the seaside. Sunday Schools, Temperance Clubs, Friendly Societies, and groups of factory workers might hire trains for special outings. In 1856 the cost of an excursion from Bristol to Weston was 7d. or 1s. 2d., and between five and six thousand people arrived on one day. There was really very little crowd trouble, but the presence of so many working class visitors rang alarm bells among the residents. The *Weston Gazette* deplored the arrival of 'the dregs of St. Philip's, Bedminster and other disreputable neighbourhoods'. On Whit Monday 1857 excursion trains brought five thousand trippers from Bristol and left behind another thousand for whom there were no places. By 1869 *Brown's Journal* was declaring 'war against the excursionists' whose numbers at peak times were now reaching between seven and eight thousand; it said there was a need to spread these 'unwelcome guests' along the sea front.

The Bank Holiday Act of 1871 effectively meant that any hopes of winning the war against excursionists by repelling the invasion were doomed. Numbers continued to rise. At Whitsun in 1876 ten thousand visitors arrived at Weston by rail or sea. By the end of the next decade there were estimates of eighteen thousand visitors on the Whitsun and August Bank Holidays. On such occasions the town's population temporarily doubled. Weston had, by this time, embraced the view that 'if you can't

114

beat them, join them' and its improved sea front was of course itself an attraction to trippers, just as its opponents had feared.

Universal bank holidays were a symbol of a more slowly working change. Perhaps more significant in the long run was the spread of holidays with pay, enjoyed by a growing number of lower grade office workers, shop assistants and some factory workers. Many people who had first become familiar with the resort on a Bank Holiday outing later returned on their annual week away from it all, and it was the gradual spread of the holiday habit down the social scale which produced what is probably still the commonly held view of the British seaside.

The numbers of lodging houses in the town grew to cater for the new class of staying visitor, and many ordinary working people in the resort took in lodgers to supplement the family income. Brown records in 1855 that landladies were meeting trains at the station to solicit custom, and were hanging signs outside their houses. The great tradition of the seaside landlady was born. It should be remembered that a high proportion of the local working class lodged with other working class families, as census returns reveal, so that even without summer visitors there were many terraced houses such as those in Alfred Street or Hopkins Street accommodating a dozen or more people throughout the year. In 1865 the *Weston Gazette* reported complaints of overcrowding in the common lodging houses, due to the large number of workmen staying in the town because of projects such as the new railway station, the Brean Down Fort and the harbour scheme. The local authority was urged to enforce the conditions stipulated in the licensing of these premises but was in some difficulty over how to go about it.

The *Weston Mercury* records the story of a lady who rented a drawing room and three bedrooms for her family in 1880. She was herself pregnant, and turned up with a lady companion and eleven children; subsequently her husband arrived with a male friend: a total of fifteen, with the smaller children packed into bed like sardines. It turned out that they were really two families who had pretended to be one in order to pay less for their lodgings.

Local landladies worked hard during the season. In order to make the maximum income they would often give up their own bedrooms and sleep in armchairs or on the sofa. Their children had to relinquish their beds and sleep under the kitchen table. It was the custom for lodgers to buy their own food and bring it

The Albert Boarding House at the north end of Beach Road. This was one of the larger boarding houses, in a prime position. It is now the Albert Hotel, and the original façade can be glimpsed behind later additions.

back to the house for the landlady to cook, and washing and cleaning were also expected. The 1887 Directory lists 161 lodging houses, mostly on or near the sea front; the 1903 Directory lists 265, spread all over the town. These figures are only the tip of the iceberg, however; hundreds of other families took in guests, both in the older terraced working class streets and in the newer streets of 'villas' built in the later years of the century. Allowing for the change to 'bed and breakfast', the same pattern held good until well after the Second World War.

The upper classes could still find superior lodging houses or even rent a house for the season, or they could indulge the Victorian middle class habit of staying in a hotel and enjoying a complete service. The 1887 Directory lists the following hotels: the Royal, the Imperial, the Victoria, the Railway, the Plough, the Claremont, the Queen's, and the Royal Pier. There were also three temperance hotels: Ford's and the Shaftesbury in Magdala Buildings and John Lake's at 3 Anstice Terrace (Alexandra Parade). The number of temperance hotels had risen to nine by 1903, and to seventeen by 1913.

In 1889 there were new 'commodious buildings adjacent to the County Club' in Knightstone Road where 'bath and dressing rooms are considered indispensable adjuncts to sleeping apartments'. The same year saw the celebratory dinner of the new Grand Atlantic Hotel in Beach Road, an enlargement of The College. Its 'Scottish Baronial' turrets made it a familiar feature of Weston's sea front, and with two hundred rooms it became the resort's only real Grand Hotel, fronting the new Beach Lawns and Esplanade. Its development was linked to yet another scheme involving a ferry service from New York, and indeed officers of the USS Enterprise were guests at the hotel at the opening. Nothing came of the ferry project, but the Grand Atlantic did break new ground by adopting the American system for hotels, namely a fixed daily charge for everything, so that middle class guests could combine precise budgeting with their bouts of opulence.

The large crowds at peak times caused fears among the residents about disorderly behaviour, which were not always groundless. Weston had only a tiny police force. The first Police Station was the home of the sergeant, in Plough Court off the High Street, and the lock-up adjoined his cottage. In 1859 the Weston Mercury described the conditions:

WESTON-SUPER-MARE.
𝕲𝖗𝖆𝖓𝖉 𝕬𝖙𝖑𝖆𝖓𝖙𝖎𝖈 𝕳𝖔𝖙𝖊𝖑,
FACING THE OCEAN.

This magnificent Hotel has recently been opened ; it is furnished in a most luxurious manner, and replete with every modern appliance. Very moderate charges ; *special* terms for Winter Residents.—For tariff apply to MANAGER.

WESTON-SUPER-MARE is three hours and a half by rail from London, half an hour from Bristol, and is the healthiest and most bracing watering-place in England.

SPECIAL ATTRACTIONS.

Pure Air : Direct Atlantic Breezes. Inexhaustible Supply of Water. Splendid Sea Front Promenade, two miles and a half in length. Extensive Sands—a Paradise for Children. Promenade and Landing Pier, with Pavilion. Steamboats to Cardiff and other Ports in the Bristol Channel. Boating, Sailing, and Bathing. 300 Acres of well grown Woods to ramble through. Summer and Winter Garden. Lawn Tennis Courts at the Hotel. Recreation Ground, with Best Cycling Track in England. Good Centre for Excursions to the far-famed Cheddar Stalactite Caves and Cliffs ; Wells, Llandaff, and Bristol Cathedrals ; Glastonbury Abbey and Tor ; Woodspring Priory ; Mendip and Quantock Hills, and the Bone Caverns of Banwell.

THE RATE OF MORTALITY FOR THE SEPTEMBER, 1888, QUARTER WAS 9·6 PER 1,000.

CLIMATE.

"The Climate is equable, with a mean winter temperature above that of London ; it is only 2° lower than that of Torquay, whilst the air is decidedly more bracing and less humid than the latter place, and therefore suits a different class of invalids. The cases that derive especial benefit from Weston air are those resulting from impaired nutrition, such as early stages of tubercular disease, chronic rheumatism, &c. The equable climate and extremely dry nature of the subsoil are also especially favourable to all disorders of a catarrhal character."—*Lancet.*

The so-called lock-up for Weston-super-Mare is a black hole about eight feet square with an open privy in one corner. Even the police, upon opening the door of the pestilential den of a morning, are often attacked with a sickness from the dreadful effluvia which belches forth upon them. What the wretched inmates of this horrible hole must suffer, who have been confined for some 12 or 18 hours, our readers can well imagine. The place is a disgrace to any civilised community – no man of feeling would permit his dog to lie therein.

A public outcry followed this report, and at the investigation which followed the Poor Law medical officer reported that there was only one cell, in which as many as five people had to spend the night. The sexes could not be segregated. The cell was open to the public sewer, and the only light and ventilation came from a small aperture 18 inches by six and from perforations in the door. One sergeant had died and the families of other officers on the premises were continually ill. The town's police force numbered three men.

The Commissioners offered the use of the basement of the newly built Town Hall. There were only two cells here, not much better than the old lock-up, but they had to serve until Divisional Headquarters were finally moved from Axbridge to a new Police Station in Oxford Street in 1891. Even the new station had only three cells, and the Weston force had only eight men, rising to fifteen by 1898. Bank Holidays brought chaos, with free fights in the streets. 'The presence of the police in the town on Monday was to a great extent a matter of form,' said the *Weston Mercury* after one such incident.

In 1844 Westonians had petitioned the House of Lords to limit the number of beer houses in the town, and there is no doubt that drunkenness was a problem which exacerbated crowd trouble at holiday times as numbers of trippers rose. Weston had nearly forty public houses at the end of the 1880s, as well as other beer houses or 'Tom and Jerry shops'. Cider was much more in evidence than it is today, and the lethal effects of the local scrumpy probably found many visitors unprepared. One can still see a number of Weston's Victorian public houses in the streets of the town centre, and for all the ill effects of drink they were important institutions among the resort's working class; the landlords were often leading figures in community life.

The ready availability of drink in the days before modern

Public houses in the town centre, links with the past. Above, Quantocks in Regent Street was formerly the Railway Hotel; the first railway station was immediately to the right. Below, the courtyard of the Britannia in North High Street, frequented by many of the traders from the market.

Above, the White Lion and below, The Globe, both in St James' Street. Both buildings date from the street's early development, although the ground floor elevations have been altered later. First floor bay windows were a common feature in the simple buildings of the early town centre streets.

licensing laws, and the inadequacy of the police force, make it surprising that there was not more serious trouble than there was in the resort. Most photographs of Bank Holiday crowds taken during these years make everyone seem extremely sober and well behaved. The seaside was the great escape for working people from the country's industrial heartlands; inevitably they brought urban habits with them. Part of the attraction of places like Weston was a relative classlessness and anarchy compared to the regimentation and caste system of the factory town, a rare break from the normal routine of long hours of repetitive work. Some exhilaration and indulgence was inevitable, the natural reaction of the deprived city worker to the seaside environment during temporary release, and not necessarily evidence of inveterate bad habits.

Local people worked long hours too, at some times of the year at least, and at other times they might not have the means to drink too much even if they had the disposition. The great local celebration when ordinary Westonians could let their hair down was the 'Wessun Revel', held on the first Thursday after 24th June. The date suggests that it may have developed from an old village fair associated with the Quarter Day or Midsummer. The Hotel Field, where the Italian Gardens are now, was the scene of this festivity for many years and saw donkey races, gingerbread and sweet stalls, travelling shows and similar attractions. Rufus Palmer remembered that 'on these occasions, treacle pies, ginger beer, spice, nuts, and gilded gingerbread besides dolls and fancy goods, to say nothing of Punch and Judy, appeared in all their glory. We youngsters looked forward to the Wessun Revel for months'.

The growing town attracted other occasional entertainments that sometimes had a topical flavour. Palmer recalled a penny peepshow visiting the resort soon after the Indian Mutiny; it had pictures of the atrocities committed by the Sepoys, and of the battles and famous generals. The showman described the events, no doubt in lurid terms.

Gradually, as Weston catered for more and more crowds, attractions became established on the beach. There were more stallholders and showmen every year, for whom the wide expanse of sand was a ready-made setting. A few alfresco shows had been staged there in the 1840s, and after the Revel moved there some of its ingredients became semi-permanent fixtures during the summer. The beach became a noisier and busier place. The completion of the Sea Front Improvement Scheme in

122

The beach as a market and funfair: crowds and stalls at the turn of the century.

the 1880s helped spread the growing crowds and also provided a viewing platform from which visitors could enjoy the bustle of the scene below. By the end of the century the beach in season was thronged with pierrots, black and white minstrels, fortune tellers, Punch and Judy, photographers, refreshment stalls, the Salvation Army, temperance speakers, performing animals and souvenir stalls.

Like other aspects of the new popular market, this caused some concern. In 1881, for example, Brown complained that the Aunt Sally and wild beast shows on the beach were a disgrace to the town. The Commissioners had only recently acquired powers of regulation over the beach to low water mark in 1876. Previously the foreshore rights had been vested in the Lord of the Manor, and the Pigotts' agent had followed a policy of being 'easy' with stallholders. The congestion resulting from unlimited numbers of stalls led the Commissioners, and subsequently the Urban District Council, to introduce a system of licensing, but this was only gradually enforced. Sunday trading was forbidden. The stalls were mostly wheeled, and were often covered with striped awnings. In the seasons leading up to the First World War thirty stalls were licensed, still enough to make up the equivalent of a considerable fair or market. The central 'pitch' was opposite the ends of Oxford Street and Richmond Street, the part of the beach for which visitors arriving at the railway station would make a beeline, and this area remained the busiest part of the sea front in later years.

The crowds brought a greater air of informality during the later years of the nineteenth century, and, if one could no longer hope to enjoy romantic solitude in Weston Bay, there was still plenty of room away from the busy central area for those who wanted a quieter time. The 'Little Sands' in Glentworth Bay remained rather more genteel than the main beach, and Anchor Head remained a favourite area for children to scramble about exploring the rock pools for crabs. The new promenade, linked to the carriage road through Weston Woods to Kewstoke, made it easier for visitors to venture further from the heart of town, and in 1890 a bus service was introduced, with fares of 1d. and 2d. Weston's shoreline offered a range of seaside experiences, and despite the more urban tone of the main sands one could still simply spend time enjoying being by the sea. The presence of dogs and small children guarantees plenty of free entertainment and mild diversion, as Jacques Tati's films remind us.

Bathing was as important as ever, although subject to more regulation. Bathing machines continued in use throughout the last century, but there were always people who preferred not to use them. In 1848 there had been complaints of men bathing naked near the ladies' machines. Bye-laws of 1869 permitted men to bathe without machines south of a fixed point on the main beach. However no one was to bathe within 200 yards of the opposite sex. Bathers were to use machines if within a quarter of a mile of a dwelling house, and the machines for men and women were to be segregated and kept 200 yards apart. Attempts to enforce these rules strictly must have involved difficult feats of calculation during busy periods. Some arrests were made but, like other efforts to regulate the changing situation, these were only partly effective. One of those who disliked the regime of bathing machines was the Revd Francis Kilvert, who stayed at Prince's Buildings in 1872. On 4th September he wrote in his diary: 'Bathing in the morning before breakfast from a machine. Many people were openly stripping on the sands a little further on and running down into the sea, and I would have done the same but I had brought down no towels of my own'. The next day he joined the rebels: 'I was out early before breakfast this morning bathing from the sands. There was a delicious feeling of freedom in stripping in the open air and running down naked to the sea, where the waves were curling white with foam and the red morning sunshine glowing upon the naked limbs of the bathers'. When the machines were destroyed or damaged in the bad gale of 1903 they were not replaced, and had clearly already become old fashioned.

Donkeys were a perennial part of the sea front scene. In village days they had been used as beasts of burden, being cheaper than horses, and among the early visitors their use was by no means restricted to children. It was common for ladies and the less dashing gentlemen to hire donkeys for quite extensive forays around the neighbouring countryside. Donkey carriages were popular with the elderly or infirm, as well as with children. Horses increasingly took over the local transport of goods, whether for the town's shops, collecting goods from the railway station, or hauling coal from Knightstone Harbour. Gentlemen rode horses, and indeed part of the attraction of the beach in the earlier and less cluttered years was the fact that the wide expanse of level open sands afforded a rare opportunity for a real gallop. Only the most aristocratic mansions had their own stables, but

Donkeys and bathing machines were two vital ingredients of the late Victorian beach scene.

the town was full of stables and mews from which horses could be hired or where they could be kept.

The donkeys became specialists in seaside entertainment, and appealed to the new crowds, who might not be very expert horsemen, as the chance for 'a bit of fun'. The growing army of donkey boys were a continual source of worry, as we have seen, and they had only seasonal employment. At the turn of the century there were up to a hundred donkeys on the beach and their stands were all along the sea front. Nowadays bye-laws give the poor patient animals some protection by decreeing a six day week, limiting rides to children, and limiting the distance of each ride to 100 yards and back.

Live music was another essential ingredient. In 1857 there had been a demand for a promenade band to enable Weston to compete with Weymouth, and within a few years German and Italian Brass Bands were playing at numerous venues in the resort. Ellenborough Park often had band concerts. Concert parties were also very popular and could be found at Grove Park, Birnbeck Island, Madeira Cove, Clarence Park, and the Assembly Rooms. In the early years of this century the outstanding figure was Henry Mogg, a former postman and self-taught musician who became proprietor of the Castle Coffee House, a well known working mens' meeting place in Castle Street, off Oxford Street. Mogg's Military Band had a long and glorious history, and won the 1912–13 national challenge shield at the Crystal Palace.

A great many people earned their livings from all these attractions and entertainments: either their main livings or a useful bit of extra pocket money. But this crowded, jolly and lively scene lives on only in old photographs or ancedotes. The stalls and booths and makeshift stages were ephemeral, swept away over the years as they were always liable to be swept away by the high tides. The very first theatre in Weston was in a tent

Beach entertainers from 1896.

pitched on land between The Boulevard and Palmer Street. In the crowded resort of the late Victorian and Edwardian years such attractions sprang up in a moment, whenever an enterprising trader or showman saw his chance; it was the people rather than the accommodation that mattered, and if this was all part of the change to an urban market, at least it brought out the best features of town life in an age when conditions in towns and cities were all too often grim and depressing. Here was colour, variety, life, which added to the resort's character and gave a necessary counterpoint to the decorous stillness of the respectable suburbs.

Open air sports had become more popular in the second half of the century, and flourished at the seaside. Tennis became popular, and many of the larger villas had private courts. In August 1888 the Lawn Tennis Championships, believed to be the first in Weston, were held on the courts of the new Grand Atlantic Hotel. The Beach Lawns had represented a victory for those wanting more space for cricket and other games. Bowls also had a following, and greens were provided in Clarence and Ashcombe parks. The Uphill Golf Club opened in 1892. Late Victorian Weston offered an impressive range of sporting opportunities to visitors and residents alike.

Entertainments began to be housed in more permanent accommodation. In 1882 the Summer and Winter Gardens opened on the north side of The Boulevard. They had a large promenading area under glass, reached through a very conspicuous entrance lodge reminiscent of a triumphal arch and designed by Hans Price. Beside the glassed area was the Victoria Hall and Opera House, capable of holding 800 people. This seems a determined effort to keep up the tone, but by the early years of the new century this private venture had been converted to a roller skating rink, with a cycling track, bowling green and tennis courts. The green was eventually bought by a bowling club which still uses it, and another part of the site was sold for a Masonic Hall. The Summer and Winter Gardens became a Palace of Varieties, then a theatre run by Carlton Fredericks, and finally the Tivoli Cinema, after substantial rebuilding. It was bombed in 1942 and remained derelict for forty years until redeveloped as flats in 1983–4.

The early years of the new century saw Knightstone Island turned into a major new attraction. Beside the original Georgian Bath House handsome new public baths were built. They used

The public baths at Knightstone. The huge settling tank beneath also extends under part of the pavilion.

sea water, taken in at high tide into a huge settling tank which is 'inside' the island. Part of the island is 'made ground' won by levelling the surface and taking in additional space with the retaining wall. The tank extends under the pavilion or theatre, which opened on the same day as the baths, 13th May 1902. Both developments were undertaken by the local authority, which had acquired the island. J.S. Stewart was the architect of the Pavilion, and Krauss the engineer, who gave it 'practically indestructible foundations'. The pavilion is 99 feet by 67 feet, and had refreshment rooms, a reading room and billiard room 'to be popular with all classes'. There were four staircases and galleries. It was planned originally for promenade band concerts, and at first good bands were engaged: the Grenadiers, the Coldstream Guards, the Horse Guards, and the White and Blue Viennese Bands. There were also plays and light opera. However the stage was too shallow for large productions. The building had electric light (a new convenience in the resort) and hot water heating. In the gale of 1903 the electrician was drowned and an audience of three hundred marooned when the causeway was

WESTON-SUPER-MARE·NEW·PIER· · ·
· · ·AND·GRAND·PAVILION·ETC·

A sketch of the proposed Grand Pier showing its intended length.

swept away during a performance. The island and causeway formed almost a second pier, and performances on a gentle summer evening here must have seemed almost magical. Afterwards one could stroll along the promenade moving from one pool of gaslight to the next.

Almost immediately a second real pier opened, the Grand Pier opposite Regent Street, and this posed stiff competition for Knightstone and Birnbeck. An Act of Parliament for a second pier had been obtained in 1893. Eventually £200,000 was subscribed for the venture and Messrs. Mayoh and Haley began erecting the iron columns in 1903. The superstructure consisted of steel openwork girders with traceried braces, and the whole pier was completed quite quickly. In June 1904 the first 360 yards and the pavilion were opened, and two years later a further 500 yards had been added. The Grand Pier was intended to receive steamers: hence the tremendous length in the centre of the bay. In fact only three boats ever called. There was silting in the approach channels, and the currents were difficult. Steamer captains refused to land here. In 1914 the original company was compulsorily wound up, and two years later the

130

The original entrance to the Grand Pier; and below a detail of the structure. *Andrew Eddy.*

extension was dismantled except for a length of forty yards beyond the pavilion.

The Grand Pier was virtually the last great pleasure pier built in this country. It eventually flourished as an entertainment centre. It was sited in the thick of the crowds, and boasted two refreshment rooms, shops, and a permanent bandstand as well as its pavilion. Entrance was 2d. and the attractions in the early years included opera, music hall, musical comedy, Shakespearean drama, ballet, as well as more 'popular' attractions such as boxing or roller skating. Mogg's Band was booked permanently for the bandstand and Herr Kandt's Austrian Band for the Pavilion. The Grand Pier relieved the pressure on the busiest section of the sea front by providing an extension of it, and it underlined the fact that the resort's appeal now rested to an important extent on its wide and varied repertoire of live entertainment.

WHAT TO SEE

● Grand Atlantic Hotel, Beach Road.

● Royal Pier Hotel, below Prince Consort Gardens.

● Pubs: Britannia, North High Street; Quantocks, Regent Street; White Lion and The Globe, St James' Street; Town Crier (Bristol and Exeter), Oxford Street.

● Swimming Baths and Pavilion, Knightstone.

● Grand Pier opposite Regent Street.

Between the Wars

Things were never quite the same after the First World War. There was a new ethos, at the seaside as elsewhere: buildings, clothes, leisure habits all changed, and Weston adapted to the 'Age of the Common Man'. There was still a sense of style, but it no longer derived from the traditional sources.

New buildings used different materials and techniques. The most obvious change was that local stone was hardly ever used; brick became the standard material, although pottery roof tiles were still in evidence. Houses built after 1918 no longer displayed a local character. We see the beginning of the housing type that is interchangeable between one town or city and another. Although Weston's population actually fell in the 1920s (the only decade in the town's history when it has done so) there was much new building during the inter-war years. Many of the new semi-detached houses were pebble-dashed or rendered over the brick. There was ribbon development along Locking Road, and considerable expansion to the south and east of the old town. Houses were built more to the scale of the ordinary modern family, and individual examples are often attractive, with interesting decorative features such as stained glass; but, taken in the mass, they are less remarkable than the resort's earlier housing.

Some examples are worth mentioning. At Milton Green the local authority built the first public housing anywhere in the country, following Addison's Act of 1919: a distinct suburb grafted onto the old hamlet of Milton, with a road layout reflecting the enlightened theories of the day that separated access roads from the main traffic thoroughfares. Subsequent council housing in this neighbourhood helped close the gap between Weston and Worle. Scattered about the town are a small number of private houses that adopt the 1930s fashion for a Mediterranean look: white painted render, interesting metal-framed windows, and in some cases flat roofs. They show that

Council housing at Milton Green, showing the new approach to road layout.

Private houses of the 1930s in Station Road: a break with older styles and materials.

some people were able to reinterpret Weston's Italianate setting in a new way.

The Town Quarry was busier than ever, but mainly supplied material for the roads. As well as producing tons of rubble it met an increased demand for tarmac, as more and more roads were upgraded for motor vehicles. The period also saw the development of Henry Butt's quarry at Milton, and indeed the emergence of Butt himself as a dominating figure on the local stage. He was the quintessential 'local boy made good', who had come to Weston as a teenager from Langport, working for a local coal company. Within a few years he had hired a horse and cart and laid the foundations of his own prosperous carrier's business, dealing in coal, building materials, and general goods. He branched out to buy the Milton Quarry, and installed giant modern kilns which produced lime for cement and whitewash. Butt also became a builder in his own right, specialising in the conversion of larger Victorian villas into 'mansions' of flats, adding wings to the original buildings. These extensions still used stone, and often the original windows were reused, so that one has to look twice to see what has happened. Many of the villas along the hillside were adapted by Butt in this way – a sign of the times.

Henry Butt lived at 1 Eastfield Park, and became a Justice of the Peace, a County Councillor, and a millionaire who gave away vast sums to charity. He entered into local mythology: the successful rough diamond who retained the common touch and never acquired the polish or style of the older élite. He would always carry cheap cigarettes which he gave out to his workmen, and pocketfuls of imitation jewellery which he gave to them for their wives. He was cordially detested by some sections of the local establishment, but there was no arguing with his drive or his money. Perhaps he brought home to the 'good' families how times were changing.

Butt was the driving force behind the local fund raising that made possible the building of the new General Hospital in The Boulevard. He personally spent many hours tramping round the town collecting donations or promises of money, ominously producing his famous black book in which to record a victim's response to his special combination of persuasion and blackmail. The hospital was practically the last major building in the town centre to use stone. It was opened by the Duke and Duchess of York (later King George VI and Queen Elizabeth) in

Henry Butt, a dominant figure in Weston between the wars.

Lime kilns at Butt's Quarry at Milton.

1927, and greatly extended the original Alfred Street buildings
with which it connected. The new hospital had balconies
opening off the wards, where convalescent patients could enjoy
the sun and air. According to local legend Butt lost the chance of
a knighthood at the opening when he lit a cigarette and blew
smoke in the Duchess's face.

Butt had engaged in a long drawn-out law suit with the Council
concerning the damage caused by his heavy vehicles to the
town's roads. His vehicles followed a triangular route between
Milton Quarry, the Goods Station, and Knightstone Harbour
where they collected coal. Butt fought the case all the way to the
House of Lords, but lost. His reaction in defeat was wholly
typical: as though to show no hard feelings he offered to meet the
cost to the town of acquiring the Hotel Field between High Street
and the sea front for the purposes of laying out the new Winter
Gardens, a project which had been long debated in the town. The
work began in 1924 and cost £16,000. The pavilion was built in

The Winter Gardens pavilion.

1927 at a cost of £35,000; the low profile of the domed building was the result of negotiations over covenants enjoyed by properties on the opposite side of the High Street since the time of the Enclosure Act, which protected their sea views.

The Winter Gardens and Pavilion were one of a number of bold steps taken by the Council during the inter-war years to fight back against the effects of nationwide recession, which took an immediate toll at the resort. One wonders if the lessons of the Sea Front Improvement Scheme of the 1880s were consciously called to mind. The new pavilion suited the leisure tastes and mood of the time, and became very popular as a venue for dancing and light orchestral concerts. The H.C. Burgess Orchestra was formed in 1920 for the summer season, and became permanent, playing regularly in the Winter Gardens pavilion until 1938.

In 1929 the Council completed another scheme, the creation of the Marine Lake at Glentworth Bay through the building of a causeway from Knightstone. Together with the older causeway to the island this trapped the tide and helped overcome the

Building the Marine Lake causeway at Glentworth Bay in 1929; a job creation scheme in action.

disappointment which the ebbing tide had always caused to many visitors. This, too, was in tune with the popular mood. There was a new relaxed informality about dress and behaviour. Sun bathing and beach parties had become fashionable, following the new life style of the smart set of the South of France. Modern girls not only cut their hair short and raised their hemlines – they bought bathing costumes that revealed the whole figure. The Marine Lake was equipped with a diving stage, rafts, rubber air boats, water chutes, children's paddle boats, as well as hundreds of bathing tents and dressing enclosures. It was dedicated to fun. The whole project had been undertaken as a job creation scheme to help relieve unemployment in South Wales. Admission to the lake was supposed to be controlled and one paid to go in and use the facilities. The Rozel bandstand was added in 1937, a further extension of the colonnaded walkway around the edge of the lake by the promenade; it replaced

139

Bathers at the Marine Lake on the concrete walkway, which was added, with a colonnaded extension to the promenade above, in 1937.

smaller and rather inadequate facilities for bands on this spot. Following gale damage in 1981 the whole of this extension was demolished and the Victorian sea wall restored.

The Knightstone Pavilion offered cinema shows, plays, light opera and other shows during the 1920s. It attracted many repertory and touring companies. Rex Harrison, Paul Robeson, and Dame Clara Butt were among those who played here. The Grand Pier added amusements to its attractions in 1926, but its days as a venue for live entertainment were ended by a devastating fire in 1930. The pier was subsequently bought by Leonard Guy, who had held the sideshows concession earlier and had been manager of the entertainments at Birnbeck. In 1932 rebuilding started above deck, but this time it was a funfair, not a theatre, that emerged. It was the largest funfair on any pier.

Weston had four cinemas by the end of the 1930s. The Winter and Summer Gardens in The Boulevard had been substantially rebuilt as the Tivoli in 1928, and there were also the Gaumont in

The new pavilion on the Grand Pier, built after the fire of 1930 had destroyed the original.

Regent Street and the Central in Oxford Street. Most distinguished of all was the Odeon, the only survivor, built on the site of the old Electric Cinema in 1935. The architect was Cecil Howitt, who won an award for the design. The building is uncompromisingly of its period, with clean lines and simple shapes: a total rejection of the Victorian notion of what a public building should look like. The external cladding tiles also proclaim modernity. Yet the building was carefully designed for its corner site facing the open space of The Plantation, and its low tower, with flat projecting top raised on short round pillars, is a strong feature. Inside, the auditorium (now subdivided) was dominated by the illuminated console of the Compton organ, which was often used for recitals and broadcasts.

Adjoining the Odeon is The Centre (rather hopefully named) facing Oxford Street, a curving row of shops which covered ground that had been open between the 1860s railway station

141

Town centre architecture of the 1930s: above, Cecil Howitt's Odeon; below, Burtons in High Street. Both buildings are actually variations on themes used throughout the country by new national companies.

The clocktower of the Grammar School, now Broadoak School.

and the Town Hall. Unfortunately many of the details that were crucial to its design have been changed. Across the corner down Walliscote Road is the Police Station and Magistrates Court, a Classical Revival building of 1934. There are some interesting shops at the south end of the main part of the High Street, on the west side, which add to the variety of the street; Burtons, on the corner with Regent Street, is especially good. At the south end of the town and facing the timbered grounds of Uphill Castle is the Grammar School (now Broadoak School) of 1935, with its central clock tower and quadrangles. This replaced temporary premises in Nithsdale road, used since the school's foundation in 1922.

These various buildings of the period hardly constituted a major change in the appearance of the town, which remained much as it had been before the First World War. The real changes were about people, and it was in the sphere of recreation, and above all along the sea front, that this was evident. The Open Air Pool was built by the council in 1937 and was the biggest in Europe. It had an Olympic standard 10 metre diving

The diving stage of the Open Air Pool was one of the most striking exponents of the modern style at Weston. It was demolished when the pool was remodelled as the Tropicana Leisure Centre.

stage in reinforced concrete, which dominated the enclosed space. Under the diving stage the pool was nearly five metres deep. The pool held 850,000 gallons of purified sea water – and 1500 bathers. There was also space for hundreds of sunbathers and spectators. In the early 1980s the diving stage was demolished and the pool was redesigned as the Tropicana Leisure Centre.

The crowds were bigger than ever during these years, and grew throughout the period. At the beginning of the 1920s August Bank Holiday crowds might number 50,000, but by the end of the next decade they were nudging 80,000. There were more lodging houses than ever, stretching back down Locking Road. Charabancs and coaches brought more and more passengers, and were available for trips from the resort. In 1928 the mansion of Belvedere in Beach Road was demolished to make way for a Bus Station. Trams ran along the sea front and back to their depot in Locking Road. They had appeared in 1902, the year after electricity came to the resort. At first there was spirited competition from the cabbies whose horses had had the sea front traffic to themselves, but the trams won, only to face stiffer competition from the buses, which finally got the upper hand. The trams disappeared in 1937, leaving fond memories.

The private motor car was still relatively scarce, but it was growing in numbers, and many of the ancient lanes between the villages around Weston were straightened and widened to cater for increased motor traffic. The old route over the hill from Uphill to Bleadon was superseded by a cutting through the hill and a new section of road by-passed the village. The village of Locking was by-passed. Yet the railway still brought the majority of visitors. Excursion trains left Bristol every few minutes at peak periods, and hundreds flooded into Locking Road from the excursion platforms that stretched back from the goods station. The enjoyment of travel, and the chance to use more unusual forms of transport, had always been part of the seaside experience; anticipation adds to any pleasure. Railway travel had been special for many Victorian visitors, who hardly stirred from their own neighbourhoods for most of the year, and no doubt the same was still true for many during the inter-war years.

There was certainly enjoyment to be derived from travelling on the Weston, Clevedon and Portishead Light Railway, which ran between 1897 and 1941. The 'Blackberry Line', as it was called, was the subject of much merriment, and can certainly be said to have epitomised a more leisurely age of travel. The Weston Station was at the junction of Milton Road and Ashcombe Road, attempts to bring it into The Boulevard having met with problems, and the line ran out to Milton and Worle, with two level crossings over the main Bristol Road, before heading off across the Northmarsh to Clevedon. Some of the miscellaneous collection of locomotives boasted observation platforms. The line was extremely useful for local people, and carried freight as well as passengers; it carried coal and collected the milk churns from isolated farms along the route, stopping at tiny stations such as Ham Lane and Wick Wharf. Like other light railways it was killed by cars and buses. With the benefit of hindsight we can see that it would now be a valuable tourist attraction if it had survived, especially as it would have served Weston's modern suburbs at Worle.

The development of bigger sea front attractions consolidated the popular image of the resort, just as it tended to fix the whole concept of the English seaside, a concept that survives to the present day. In consequence, the original importance of the town's setting and the pleasures to be obtained from easy access to attractive countryside began to fade from the picture. Nevertheless, until the Second World War, and for some years afterwards, Weston was a place where the visitor might still be aware of the rural hinterland. One could walk out to open countryside within ten or fifteen minutes from anywhere in the town. The popular writer S.P.B. Mais began his chapter on Weston in *Walking in Somerset* (1935):

> Weston-super-Mare is at once one of the most amusing and most picturesque of popular seaside resorts. It is in consequence roundly abused by those who have never visited it. It is easily accessible by air, sea and land, and makes a very good centre for excursions to all parts of Somerset. It is, for instance, the obvious starting point for the Mendip Hills.

In an era when the rights of popular access to the countryside were at last established, after battles in the nineteenth century and campaigns by the Ramblers Association, there were indeed many enthusiastic hikers and ramblers who emulated Mais and explored the country around Weston. The walk to Kewstoke and Sand Bay was popular, perhaps including the tea garden at the top of Monk's Steps. One might venture beyond Uphill, use the

146

ferry at the mouth of the Axe to cross to Brean, and talk to Harry Cox in his hut on Brean Down; Cox acted as warden of the headland and its wildlife for more than a quarter of a century. Or one could head inland to explore the still undeveloped villages of Hutton, Locking and Worle. Despite new farming methods and road transport, the countryside around the resort was far less touched by modernity than the town itself, and the old rural way of life subsisted practically on Weston's doorstep.

Nevertheless the value of the town's setting was ceasing to be appreciated by all its citizens, as became evident when Weston Woods came under threat. The Smyth Pigott estate had been steadily selling off land since the turn of the century, disposing of farms by auction. It had retained the woods throughout this period, although they had been open for public enjoyment since the middle of the nineteenth century; very occasionally they were closed for a day in order to preserve the estate's legal rights. In 1936 nearly four hundred acres of the woods were offered to the local authority for £10,000 but the deal was turned down. Soon afterwards the land was sold to a syndicate for £19,500. A broad road along the top was opened from the eastern end to the water tower, and it was planned to build houses along the top of the hill. Eventually the Council was shamed into action and managed to acquire less than three hundred acres for £22,500, together with a section of the Jackson-Barstow estate at Ashcombe. Most of the woods were saved, but it was impossible to stop building at the eastern end.

1936 also saw the opening of the Weston airfield to the east of the town on Locking Moor, a development that was less detrimental to the local environment and put it briefly on the world map in terms of aviation. It had important repercussions on the later history of the town. Colonel S.F. Cody had brought the first aeroplane to Weston in 1911, landing on the beach in front of the Grand Atlantic, and in the same year Mr B.C. Hucks made the first of a number of flights across the Bristol Channel. Small planes used the sands or nearby fields for landing and take-off frequently in the following years. In the 1930s the Council gave approval for the building of a municipal airport, which was soon leased to Western Airways, and a brief period of cross-Channel flights began. These were immediately popular, and the service was taken over by the Straight Corporation in 1938. Whitney Straight was a pioneer of domestic air services, and under his direction the operation was expanded. New routes were added, even including occasional flights to Paris. On 2nd October 1938 the first internal night service began, with floodlights on the airfield. The service to Cardiff was by now half-hourly, which was claimed to be the most frequent anywhere in the world. Weston airfield was the second busiest in the country. However in 1939, with war looming, the Air Ministry established a reserve centre at Weston, and the following year, after war had been declared, the Weston-Cardiff service was closed despite local objections. The fleet of aircraft, including De Havilland and Dragon biplanes, was requisitioned, and Weston's brief career as a major civilian aviation centre was ended.

The Urban District Council, which had replaced the Commissioners, was itself replaced by a Borough Council in 1937. Weston was now a proper town, with its own mayor and corporation. The charter was presented in front of a large crowd at the Grove Park bandstand, and the first Mayor of Weston-super-Mare was, almost inevitably, Henry Butt. The proud new borough took as its motto 'Ever Forward', and it must certainly have seemed as if the momentum of improvement and expansion was assured and unstoppable. The crowds would go on getting bigger than ever, the sun would shine in a cloudless sky, and the money would roll in. Yet at the very moment of achieving its coveted borough status Weston was set to encounter problems. As the controversy over the woods had presaged, the high point of civic pride and complacence contained the seeds of future difficulties. These were not to become apparent for some years, but in many respects, this was Weston's finest hour.

WHAT TO SEE

- Milton Green: first council houses.

- Private houses in Station Road; Cecil Road.

- Winter Gardens Pavilion.

- Odeon Cinema.

- Shops at south end of main High Street.

- Airfield buildings by Locking Moor Road.

Modern Times

The runway of Weston Airfield was built during the Second World War, when the town saw a rapid build-up of plant connected with wartime aviation needs. RAF Locking had begun as a hutted camp in 1938 and trained personnel in many skills. There were several 'shadow factories' near the airfield. The Western Airways site became a factory producing aircraft and employing three hundred local people: the twin engine canvas-covered Avro Anson 'bone-shakers', used by the RAF for pilot training, were built here. Bristol Aircraft Ltd. produced Bristol Beaufighters at their Oldmixon factory, and during the war 3400 aircraft were built. The airfield itself was never 'operational' in a combat sense, although it was a reserve site, and drainage

Bristol Beaufighter production at Weston during World War Two. *British Rotorcraft Museum.*

improvements were carried out to the Uphill Great Rhyne to protect the area. A new pumping station was built to ensure that the area remained free of flooding.

Important research was undertaken along the Weston coast. Birnbeck Pier became 'H.M.S. Birnbeck' and new weapons were tested here, as well as at Brean Down Fort and St. Thomas's Head at Middle Hope. These included the 'bouncing bomb' devised by Barnes Wallis and used by the Dambusters, which was to prove critical in defeating the threat posed by the German U-boats. Anti-aircraft batteries, part of a ring protecting Bristol and the Channel approaches, were located near Weston. One can still see the remains of some of these on Brean Down. Weston Woods was also used, and was out of bounds to local people for some time. In addition there were measures to prevent a beach landing by the enemy, with mines and barbed wire barricades. Weston's own 'Dad's Army', the Home Guard, occupied the same hilltop sites which had been look-out spots and beacon sites centuries before. The old windmill tower at Uphill was one observation post.

Weston may have gained a reputation in Germany as a munitions town, and some have attributed bombing raids on the town to this fact. The first bombs fell on Weston in 1940, but the first major air raid came on 4th January 1941, when thirty-four people were killed and eighty-five injured. Rector's Way, Stonebridge Road, Grove House, St. Paul's Church and Whitecross Hall were among the sites hit, together with other shops and houses. Even more damage was caused the following year, on 28th and 29th June, when ten thousand incendiaries and over sixty high explosive bombs fell on the town. Over a hundred people were killed and four hundred were injured. The Tivoli Cinema, the Lance and Lance store on the High Street-Waterloo Street corner, the Boulevard Congregational Church, the Wadham Street Baptist Church, the Assembly Rooms and Marks and Spencer in the High Street were all hit, together with 3500 houses damaged or destroyed. These raids were blamed by some on an article in the *News Chronicle* shortly before, which had reported a display of war weapons staged on the sea front for munitions workers from all over the country. There were further raids in 1944.

On 1st August 1942, after the worst raid, the *Weston Gazette* headlined its reports and photographs of the local bomb damage with the stirring declaration 'From these ruins a still fairer town shall rise.' However it was some years after the war before the

Second World War bomb damage to a Victorian villa, above, and below, the interior of St. Paul's church after an air raid. *Weston Mercury.*

151

bomb sites were redeveloped. As in most British towns and cities during the Age of Austerity these sites remained derelict, some of them (such as the Tivoli, Oxford Street, and the Grove Park-Wadham Street sites) serving as car parks.

Nevertheless the post-war period saw an infectious optimism for bold redevelopment projects, and a new breed of professional planners who began turning out radical blueprints for our towns and cities. Such a scheme was prepared for Weston in 1947 at the Borough Council's request, by Clough Williams-Ellis and Lionel Brett. It revealed the extent to which modernism was prepared to go in reshaping the Victorian resort. The report was enthusiastic about 'Weston's wonderful assets, some of them unique' but devoted most space to discussing ways of 'consistently and imaginatively exploiting them':

> the possible embellishments are almost endless, quite apart from the general layout and structure of the town itself, the rational recasting of which to give comeliness and convenience is, of course, the first basic priority.

The Beach Road frontage 'is wholly unworthy, and we put forward as one method of redevelopment a series of eight-storey hotels and blocks of flats'. The Shrubbery 'remains an asset to Weston' but is most important as 'an invitation to imaginative private enterprise. Similar areas in London . . . have been found ideal for redevelopment'. Ellenborough Park should be extended eastward to a new railway station square, and at its seaward end there could be a conference hall and restaurant overlooking the bay.

The report seized on the fact that the future belonged to the motor car and proposed three new arterial roads which would slice up the town and speed the motorist on his way to the beach or the town centre. Very little happened, because of the state of the national economy and the difficulties experienced locally in obtaining the necessary war damage compensation, but this local monument to the new planning philosophy continued to be invoked in support of some of the less grand schemes that actually began to appear in the 1960s.

Lances Corner, opposite the Italian Gardens, saw one of the first projects which revealed the further changes that had come about by this time in building materials and styles. The building line was set back to facilitate road improvements which

Lances' Corner, looking down Waterloo Street across High Street, after the air raid of 1942. *Weston Mercury*. Below, the same view today, showing the rebuilding of the 1960s.

were anticipated. The Plantation opposite Alexandra Parade was modified to form a giant traffic island, and there were demolitions around Big Lamp corner for redevelopment and road widening. Union Street was widened and rebuilt as a southern extension of High Street. There was considerable opposition to the siting of a new technical college on the corner of Lower

153

The view up Lower Church Road in the middle of the last century, with the National School on the left and Oriel Terrace beyond. Below, the view today, with the College of Further Education, formerly called the Technical College.

Church Road. The building shocked Westonians by its scale and character, and it remains the town's most unpopular building. In 1962 the Somerset county architect said that it would provide 'a really vigorous piece of punctuation in the town scene'.

Perhaps the most controversial redevelopment scheme was the Dolphin Square shopping centre between Oxford Street and Carlton Street. There had been some bomb damage in Oxford Street but most of this neighbourhood of small streets was still intact. The Council sought to realise here the concept of a conference centre, hotel and covered pool, and commissioned another report, from Chamberlin, Powels and Bon. Investment could not be attracted for the project, however, and the Council switched to a mixture of shops and flats. Existing houses were declared to be sub-standard and clearance orders were obtained; compulsory purchase orders followed, sometimes with minimal compensation. The community was split up and many residents were rehoused on the suburban council estates. They had fought a hard and bitter battle, and had found a powerful advocate in

Houses from the earlier years of Weston's resort development in Carlton Street, demolished for the Dolphin Square Shopping Centre.

One of the many small streets and courts which surrounded Carlton Street; an entire community was uprooted and some of the houses declared unfit.

the Vicar of Emmanuel, the Revd Mr Bowes, who said after the fight was lost:

> A decent little residential district has been allowed to become a shambles. Since the blitz I have seen nothing like it . . . I hope that the speedy and imaginative development of this area will justify the amount of human suffering to people whose houses have been compulsorily purchased. Otherwise, those responsible will stand morally condemned.

Development projects had been controversial on many occasions in the past, but the enhanced role of the local authority, reflecting post-war notions of planning, seemed to bring the potential for a new bitterness into local disputes.

The population in 1946 was 39,000. Growth was slow in the immediate post-war years, but the pace quickened in the 1960s. Wartime developments led to important consequences on the industrial front as well as in the town centre. Before 1939 industry had seemed to be incompatible with tourism, but the

156

The Westlands factory in Winterstoke Road, until recently the town's biggest employer.

wartime policy of dispersing factories to places such as Weston had shown local people that industry could co-exist with resort interests. The experiment, forced on the town, had been shown to work and the Council began to favour its continuation. Local leaders wished to cater for the employment needs of a larger population, and in particular to provide for local school leavers, who found few opportunities in the resort. The wartime factories had adapted to new work. At the Bristol Aircraft factory at Oldmixon a helicopter production line was established in 1956, and in 1961 the site was taken over by Westlands. The Yeovil-based company used the site for the assembly and repair of helicopters and fixed wing aircraft, as well as for the training of pilots for foreign air forces. The company became the biggest employer at Weston, with 1500 people at one time working on the 88 acre site. Eventually Westlands bought the airfield itself, which had continued to operate pleasure flights until 1978. Henly's also had a factory on the site. Both factories, however, were dependent on government contracts, and the town's unemployment problem, while alleviated, remained latent. Westlands ran into a crisis in the mid-1980s, triggering nationwide political

157

The start of helicopter manufacture at Weston in 1956: Bristol Sycamores being made for the Bristol Aircraft Company. One of the machines (the third to be built) is preserved in the British Rotorcraft Museum. Production of the model had begun at Filton in 1954; it continued at Weston until 1959. 178 were built, mainly for the British, West German and Australian military. *British Rotorcraft Museum.*

argument and the resignation of two cabinet ministers. In 1987 the company announced that 800 jobs were to be lost from the 1200 workforce. New companies have been established, employing most of those remaining, and have set about winning contracts on the open market.

In 1957 Somerset County Council produced a draft town map for Weston, containing no allocation for industrial development. The Borough Council successfully sought a change to allow for new initiatives. Taking advantage of post-war planning legislation, and the lack at that time of restrictions on local authority spending, the Council obtained loan sanction for developing a new industrial estate at Oldmixon. 130 acres were bought under the Town Development Scheme for an overspill agreement with Birmingham. 44 acres of the site were earmarked for industry. Exhibitions were staged in Birmingham in 1959 and 1961. The initiative was a success, and the estate was filled in four years.

WESTON - SUPER - MARE.

INDUSTRIAL DEVELOPMENT.

OFFERS EXCELLENT OPPORTUNITIES FOR THE LOCATION OF INDUSTRIES IN A MODERN & PROGRESSIVE SEASIDE RESORT.

1. CONVENIENT ROAD & RAIL ACCESS TO BIRMINGHAM & LONDON.
2. HOUSES PROVIDED FOR EMPLOYEES WISHING TO MOVE FROM BIRMINGHAM OR OTHER APPROVED EXPORTING AREAS.
3. EXCELLENT LEVEL SITES AVAILABLE WITH ALL SERVICES.
4. COUNCIL WILL CONSIDER ERECTION OF FACTORY PREMISES TO INDUSTRIALISTS REQUIREMENTS
5. LOW DENSITY RESIDENTIAL SITES - OWNED BY COUNCIL - AVAILABLE IN A PLEASANT AREA FOR EXECUTIVES TO BUILD ON.

Firms moving to the site included Harris Biological Supplies, Compression Joints, Philip Harris Ltd., C.H. Hare and Son Ltd., and Concargo. The Council built some of the factories itself for letting, laid out the estate, and provided the roads and sewers. The rest of the site was available for commercial facil-

159

Houses on the Oldmixon Estate of the 1960s, built in conjunction with the new factories.

Clarks' shoe factory in Locking Road.

ities and housing for key personnel. In attracting companies the Council operated restrictive policies, inspecting existing factories and their processes; it only entertained manufacturing concerns which had a high ratio of workers to square footage, and would not let space go for warehousing.

In the mid-1960s a second estate of 55 acres was planned, on the other side of Winterstoke Road next to Westlands, but this project became a casualty of the national economic downturn in the late sixties. The cost of moving became much higher, and interest rates went up. C. & J. Clark had opened a shoe factory in Locking Road in 1958, and this was followed by a second at Oldmixon. An older industry vanished, the potteries at Langford Road having finally been forced out of business by the rise of the plastic flower pot. RAF Locking had become the No. 1 Radio School in 1950, and a permanent community sprang up behind the trim hedges along the Locking by-pass, where technicians were trained to work with radio, radar and flight simulators. The station came to contain the largest complex of training computers in the RAF.

The Midlands increasingly replaced South Wales as Weston's principal catchment area. Many Midlands workers who had visited Weston on holiday were keen to move here with their companies, and the careful co-ordination of policies to provide housing for essential workers overcame employers' fears about the disincentive of an unskilled local labour force. Weston had come to terms with a 'mixed economy' of light industry and tourism, and the Council's positive action in the 1960s appeared to be producing an adequate employment base for the local population. No sooner was this goal in sight, however, than it receded again, as new developments unfolded.

Birnbeck Pier had been bought from the Pier Company by Campbells in 1962, and was sold by them to Mr John Critchley ten years later. The era of the steamers was ending, and the last steamer, the *Balmoral*, called in 1979. There were no longer enough people embarking at Weston, and the state of the steamer jetty at Birnbeck was causing concern. As the steamer service faded, the motorway began to have a major impact on the town. Weston sought to exploit its position as the nearest resort to Birmingham in terms of motor travel. The motorway was an extension of the M5 Birmingham to Bristol route, first proposed in 1961 and constructed between 1968 and 1973; it has since been extended as far as Exeter.

PROPOSED DEVELOPMENT

PRESENT BUILT UP AREA

The spread of Weston-super-Mare, 1987.

In terms of industrial development, however, Weston has not been able to realise the potential which the motorway link seemed to promise. By the time it came the national economy was entering a downturn. There were many other towns competing to attract firms that were as well placed by the new system: Swindon and the northern fringe of Bristol, in the 'M4 corridor', benefited dramatically in this respect. South Wales was a Development Area, more accessible once the Severn Bridge opened in 1966, and able to offer tax concessions. In Weston the road system between the motorway interchange and the industrial estate still represented a significant distance (in terms of travelling time), so that more accessible sites farther down the motorway could still seem more attractive.

162

On the other side of the equation, the building of the motorway helped fuel an unprecedented house building boom. Weston had been earmarked by Somerset County Council in the 1960s for major residential growth. The town spread away from its old centre towards the east and the motorway interchange, and the population grew by 20,000 within fifteen years. Worle changed from a village, surrounded by deep lanes and ancient farmsteads, to a sprawl of new estates. At one time the growth rate at Weston was one of the three or four highest in the country. Inevitably many of the new residents were commuters, working in Bristol, Avonmouth or elsewhere; one survey in the early 1980s showed that there were 900 travelling salesmen living on the Worle estates. There was much criticism of the planning and layout of the new estates, and of the slow development of neighbourhood amenities. Because all the growth had to take place in one direction, Weston became a distended town whose centre was geographically at one end of its mass. Although local groups have worked hard at Worle and Mead Vale to develop a degree of cohesion and identity in their neighbourhoods, there is a general feeling that community identity is much less strong than formerly.

House building has continued on a large scale, and has begun to arouse considerable disquiet within the town. A network of groups and parish councils formed a 'Stop the Sprawl' campaign in the 1980s to fight the County Structure Plan, and Weston's Member of Parliament, Jerry Wiggin, also called for some respite in order to give the town a breathing space. Local government reorganisation in 1974 moved Weston from Somerset to the new County of Avon, based on Bristol, despite a local referendum which revealed overwhelming opposition to the change. Time has not lessened the unpopularity of the new arrangement and there has been an active 'Back to Somerset' campaign, which still continues. Although local government reorganisation was not the prime cause of the building boom, a feeling has developed that Weston's interests count for little in the city-based authority, and the fact that the new estates at Weston are largely designed to meet the needs of people working elsewhere adds to this sentiment. The town is increasingly seen as one of Bristol's dormitory suburbs, and the new estates have little organic connection with the old resort.

Tourism has continued as a major source of employment, although here too changes have left the local economy more vulnerable. After the war crowds continued to pour into the resort, but in the 1960s the effects of the private motor car began to be felt. Greater mobility led to a decline in the numbers of staying visitors. Caravan parks covered more fields around the town, which was increasingly seen as a touring centre by many visitors. By the end of the 1970s Weston, in common with most English resorts, was facing serious difficulties. Cheap foreign travel was probably the biggest single factor; more and more people flew to destinations where the sunshine was guaranteed. People might still visit the resort for a second holdiay, or an 'impulse' weekend break, but their main holiday spending was going elsewhere. Many hotels changed over to self-catering accommodation, and, encouraged by Tourist Board grants, attempted to modernise. Rooms had to have individual bathrooms and colour televisions. There were protests that the extensions, sun lounges, and extra storeys and lift housings were spoiling some of the town's most attractive buildings in the sea front area. No new hotels were built after the war, and recently many have closed. Some have become rest homes or nursing homes for the elderly.

Other factors have been identified as causes of the resort's problems. There has been a boom in special interest holidays, for which Weston seemed ill-prepared. Peoples' tastes were more sophisticated, and, enjoying greater leisure in general, they came to their holidays with more energy and appetite for occupation. Sitting on the beach or riding a donkey was no longer enough for many. The resort never acquired the facilities or the hotel accommodation that would have enabled it to cater for major conferences. The polluted state of the estuary began to attract publicity and criticism. Heavier road traffic brought its own problems, with jams on the main road into town more frequent at peak times and calls for a new route from the motorway interchange to the town centre. The ending of steamer services removed an attraction which might have increased in appeal. The resort has become dangerously dependent on a limited section of the tourist market which is shrinking while other sectors dramatically expand. Physical changes have begun to erode the town's character, giving an impression of cheapness rather than quality, and lack of long-term reinvestment worsens the position.

Nevertheless Weston remains a major holiday centre. An English Tourist Board survey in 1978 found that 11% of the

Local government before and after reorganisation in 1974.

165

population were dependent one way or another on tourism, and updated figures suggest that tourism brings £60 million annually to the area, most of it to Weston. Good weather still brings large crowds. Weston is a popular retirement town, and many of the large Victorian villas have been converted into flats which make pleasant retirement homes. The building boom of the early 1970s saw several historic mansions demolished to make way for new tower blocks of flats (the Villa Rosa in the Shrubbery; Glentworth House opposite the Marine Lake; Etonhurst in Beach Road). The fight against proposals to build to fourteen storeys on the Etonhurst site was the local conservation movement's first major victory. It should be said that Weston has suffered far less than other major resorts such as Torquay or Brighton in this respect. Far more damage has been done to the fabric of the historic resort through clumsy alterations to old buildings.

At the time of local government reorganisation Weston became part of the new District of Woodspring, which reaches to the western side of Bristol and includes Portishead and Clevedon. The former Borough was persuaded to support merger with the area of the old Long Ashton District Council by those in the latter authority who feared being taken over by Bristol. In this way the seemingly more obvious option of a merger with the former Axbridge Rural District Council – which would have left Weston centrally placed in relation to its natural hinterland – was rejected. The need to centralise staff led to the building of a major extension to the Town Hall, opened in 1980, for which the Albert Memorial Hall behind Emmanuel Church was demolished. The estimated population of the district in 1986 was 177,800, according to the Census Office, making it the eleventh largest non-metropolitan authority in the country. The chief executive has pointed out that Woodspring is larger than two metropolitan districts which are running their own education services. About two-thirds of the councillors represent wards outside Weston. Some councillors themselves feel that the conflict of loyalties sometimes outweighs the advantages and efficiencies brought by greater size. Their interests and loyalties cannot be evenly spread across the district, and decisions about the allocation of resources have to be taken on the basis of horse trading rather than on the merits of each case. There are calls for a town of Weston's size (now approaching 70,000) to have its own council again.

The modern extension to the Town Hall, with the new main entrance which superseded that in Hans Price's building. After local government reorganisation it was decided to provide extra premises in order to centralise council staff. It was also felt that the new authority should have a new image.

Weston was too large to have a lower tier town council at reorganisation, so it is in the anomalous position of not enjoying its own elected tier of local government while villages in the district have parish councils. The Weston members of Woodspring do, however, sit as the Charter Trustees and elect the Town Mayor. The remaining section of Grove House now forms the mayor's parlour, and arrangements with the District permit the Charter Trustees to raise a local rate.

A new district hospital was opened to the east of Uphill in 1986, after many years of campaigning by local people and their councillors; Weston now forms part of the Bristol and Weston Health Authority, and there has been some resentment that Westonians have to travel to Bristol for treatment that should be available locally. Some have also questioned whether Uphill was the right place for the new hospital in view of the town's development towards the motorway, but their doubts were swamped by the general desire to get the new hospital built at all.

167

The new hospital at Uphill, opened in 1986 after a long campaign.

In 1980 the first conservation areas were designated in Weston (at Uphill, Worle, and around Grove Park and Park Place); others have subsequently been designated between Birnbeck and Queen's Road on the hillside, and at Uphill and Ellenborough Park. The move was opposed by some interest groups who feared that it would impose restraints on commercial activity. The 'conservation debate' came to the fore at the end of the 1970s, promoted by the Civic Society. Public meetings and correspondence in the *Weston Mercury* revealed public support for conservation policies, although a genuine local concensus has yet to emerge.

In 1975 the Woodspring Museum was opened in the former Gas Company offices and showrooms in Burlington Street, with collections moved from the upper floor of the library in The Boulevard. New galleries have been opened since, and in 1987 Clara's Cottage, adjoining the museum, was opened to show a typical small house as it would have been towards the end of the last century. The museum is popular with both visitors and local people, and has won national awards for the quality of its work.

The Civic Society's Heritage Centre in Wadham Strreet, opened in 1986 in a former coach house; the top floor was originally a tailor's workshop.

In 1986 the Civic Society opened the Weston Heritage Centre in a converted coach house and warehouse in Wadham Street, with displays telling the story of the town and the surrounding countryside. It also has a conservation shop which gives advice and practical help to people involved in maintaining older buildings, and is the base for a salvage scheme that rescues materials and fittings from such properties and makes them available for re-use. The society has sponsored a number of enhancement schemes in the town, and is currently involved in two major projects: converting The Blakehay, the former Wadham Street Baptist Church, into an Arts and Community Centre for the Weston-super-Mare Trust; and landscaping the Town Quarry and rehabilitating some of its buildings for new uses.

The District Council opened the Hutton Moor Leisure Centre in 1987, and Winterstoke Road has become a link in what is planned to be a new main road into town from the motorway. A new section of road, Herluin Way, connects Winterstoke Road to Hutton Moor Road and Locking Road. Thus the route of the

The Hutton Moor Leisure Centre, opened in 1987.

original branch railway line now serves the motor car, and road transport dominates thinking about these issues. The railway station has survived plans to close it in order to clear the way for the new road and replace it with a new station on the main line closer to Worle; but maintenance costs still pose a threat to the main station structure. The newly privatised Badgerline Bus Company closed the Beach Road Bus Station in 1987; it was subsequently demolished to make way for a block of flats.

Knightstone Island became a 'problem site' in the 1980s, with the Council seeking bids for its development and not ruling out the possibility of demolition of all the island's buildings. In the event no acceptable proposals were forthcoming, and the option of conservation and adaptation appears to hold the key to the future of this important sea front area.

The Borough Council's plans for economic development in the 1960s included commercial activity, but in this respect Weston failed to take off. The town was too near Bristol to be able to attract any major office development. Recent initiatives in the private sector have been in the sphere of retailing, reflecting national trends during a period of economic readjustment. Sainsburys opened a major 'out of town' store which is the

The new Tesco store in Locking Road on the site of the second railway station.

biggest element in the new District Centre at Worle, convenient for the motorway and including a large car park. Winterstoke Road has attracted several retail stores. Tesco recently opened a new store on the site of the 1860s railway station, next to the Odeon Cinema and facing The Plantation and Alexandra Parade. As the result of a deal with the District Council it has flats above it, named Hildesheim Court to mark Weston's twinning with Hildesheim in Germany. Although close to the old town centre, the new Tesco store looks like an 'out of town' development, much of the frontage giving onto a large car park.

Fears about the health of the old town as a shopping centre have grown, but the immediate future offers some hope that the balance may be redressed. Royal Life are beginning the construction of a major new covered shopping centre behind High Street and taking in the site of the General Post Office, with elevations facing the Italian Gardens and Victoria Square. Earlier proposals to attract such development by offering the gardens themselves for building led to one of the fiercest controversies in Weston for a long time. The Civic Society raised a petition of over eight thousand signatures in a fortnight, and its vision of a newly-landscaped Town Square providing the focus for a revived town centre may become a reality under the new plans. There are also plans to pedestrianise the main section of High Street (for some years there has been partial pedestrianisation), and to build a new multi-purpose conference hall next to the Winter Gardens Pavilion.

The 'conservation debate' of the last few years has been in part a reflection of Weston's uncertainty about its modern identity. Concern about the treatment of the town's buildings and open spaces is one expression of unease about the underlying trends in the resort. Westonians see a mixed picture. On one hand there have been signs of confidence and willingness to invest in the town, which is especially reflected in the retailing and service sector and is consistent with growth in the numbers of commuters and relatively wealthy retired people coming to live here; in this respect Weston participates in the region's relative prosperity. On the other hand, there remain worries about the overall balance of the town's economic base. Tourism is in relative decline, and other forms of employment have not materialised to an extent sufficient to keep pace with the needs of a growing population; Weston is an unemployment blackspot with rates well above the national and regional averages. Many of its inhabitants are personally well off, and this sustains some sectors of the local economy well; but in other respects commuters and retired people are classes which take out of a community more than they put back. Personal life styles may be cultivated while aspects of the town's communal life languish. The new estates of North Worle seem largely unconnected with the old town, which has gradually become a community of low expectations. Thus, notwithstanding some major new investments, general depreciation and lack of reinvestment have produced an overall disinvestment in recent years in the town as a whole.

Those who oppose conservation policies believe that the resort should do nothing to impede economic development, which is the engine of community well-being. Those in favour of such policies believe that regeneration is more likely to come through careful reuse of buildings in the old town rather than their destruction, and through a reaffirmation of local character and identity. They argue that quality and a distinctive image is the key to prosperity, and propose regeneration schemes of the kind

172

being launched elsewhere in the country, believing that this strategy is more likely to reconcile apparently conflicting interests within the community. Recent debates seem to echo those from the pages of local history between residents and those with tourism interests; but today the debates take place against a background of falling visitor numbers.

WHAT TO SEE

- Factories at Elborough and Oldmixon.

- 1960s development: Dolphin Square, South High Street; Technical College; District Hospital, Brigwater Road.

Retrospect

A resort, like other towns, lives off its past achievements to an extent which makes a 'snapshot' of it at any one time an imperfect indicator of its state at that moment. A community continues to take advantage of the buildings and amenities won by previous generations, whether or not it is effectively renewing itself. There is thus a factor of 'delayed action', which tends to obscure the appearance of difficulties of which only the most alert members of the community may initially be aware.

In most towns the communal life in all its aspects is so complex that simple statements about 'rise and fall' are dangerous, but in the case of a resort town like Weston it is possible to describe a clear trajectory of the community's fortunes. The loss of momentum and direction, the disappearance of a clear sense of purpose and identity, which became apparent in the post-war years, probably had their origins in the period between the First and Second World Wars.

Seaside towns can only be fully understood in the context of the wider national story; in themselves they make only partial sense. Resorts are a paradox, whose complete meaning is explained in the history of work, while they themselves are dedicated to leisure. The nature of work for most people underwent profound changes in the nineteenth century as Britain became the first modern country to exploit new technology and the methods of mass production on a wide scale. We were the first modern industrial society. The nature of peoples' everyday work influences their whole lives; it determines what they spend most of their time doing, where they live and who they meet; and it determines the character of their leisure. Seaside towns in their developed form were embodiments of Victorian England's leisure options, at first for the upper and managerial classes, later for the mass of ordinary industrial workers. The seaside was the great escape from the factories, mines and offices of industrial Britain.

The very nature of the relief they offered from new forms of work meant that they themselves should contain little industry. The whole point was that they should be different. The conscious decision after the Second World War to attract light industry seems to be an indication that the pure purpose of the resort had already disappeared at Weston. Greater mobility and foreign travel, themselves signs that modern work was changing, signalled other leisure options, and it is not yet clear whether our resorts have found a role to play in this pattern that is truly of the present day and not just a 'run on' from older habits and allegiances.

In their heyday, before the First World War, resorts embodied the confidence and optimism of the society they served. One is therefore bound to interpret their more recent uncertainty as an indicator of national fortunes. In its classic period Weston embodied the fine balance between the natural world and the complex achievements and failures of a technologically advanced society. The pilgrimage to the sea, and the respite from mechanical work, created a balance that was crucial to the nation's psyche. Here in physical form was the very meeting place between urban civilisation and the untamed energy of the waves; it was no accident, but the result of blind, deep instinct, that this became the scene of recreation and refreshment.

At Weston one still has the opportunity to trace, in unusual detail, the outline of the classic watering place, which may after all still carry its old meaning in a new form to a modern generation. Seen across the bay from Brean Down, Weston still looks very much as it did a century ago. Such a view sums up 'the logic of the landscape' as it was interpreted by the mature resort: falling down the hillside and spreading round the shore, the crisp and sharply defined details of a civilised townscape, which looks out towards the free wild spaces of the Celtic west.

SELECT BIBLIOGRAPHY

Adamson, S. 1977. *Seaside Piers.*

Aston, M. 1976. *Brean Down Fort,* Somerset County Council (typescript).

Aston, M. and Burrow, I. (eds.) 1982. *The Archaeology of Somerset.*

Aston, M. and Iles, R. 1987. *The Archaeology of Avon.*

Bailey, J. 1985. *Weston-super-Mare: The Good Old Days.*

Bailey, J. 1986. *Look Back with Laughter.*

Baker, E. 1887. *A Chronicle of Leading Events in the History of Weston-super-Mare during the past fifty years.*

Baker, E. (ed.) 1901. *John Chilcott's 1822 Guide to Weston-super-Mare.*

Baker, E. 1910. *Weston-super-Mare Parish Church, 1226 to 1910.*

Baker, E. 1911. *Weston-super-Mare: Village Jottings.*

Baker, E. 1912. *The History of Weston-super-Mare from 1326.*

Baker, E. 1928. *The Village of Weston-super-Mare: Historical Notes.*

Barrett, J. n.d. *A History of Maritime Forts in the Bristol Channel* (typescript in Woodspring Central Library).

Billingsley, J. 1797. *General View of the Agriculture of the County of Somerset.*

Branigan, K. and Fowler, P.J. (eds.) 1976. *Roman West Country.*

Brown, B.J.H. 1971. *Survey of the Leisure Industries of the Bristol Region,* unpublished Ph.D. thesis, University of Bath.

Brown, B.J.H. and Loosley, J. 1979. *The Book of Weston-super-Mare.*

Brown, B.J.H. and Loosley, J. 1985. *Yesterday's Town.*

Buchanan, A. and Cossons, N. 1969. *Industrial Archaeology of the Bristol Region.*

Buchanan, B.J. 1982. 'The Financing of Parliamentary Waste Land Enclosure: Some Evidence from North Somerset, 1770–1830', *Agricultural History Review 30.*

Burrow, I. 1976. 'Brean Down Hillfort, Somerset, 1974', *University of Bristol Spelaeological Society Proceedings 14(2).*

176

Coles, J.H. and Orme, B.J. 1982. *Prehistory of the Somerset Levels.*

Collinson, J. 1791. *The History and Antiquities of the County of Somerset.*

Costen, M. 1979. 'Place Name Evidence in South Avon', *Avon Past 1.*

Coysh, A.W., Mason, E.J., and Waite, V. 1954. *The Mendips.*

Davey, N. 1961. *A History of Building Materials.*

Day, J. 1973. *Bristol Brass: The History of The Industry.*

Dunning, R.W. (ed.) 1976. *Christianity in Somerset.*

Dunning, R.W. 1978. *A History of Somerset.*

Dymond, C.W. 1902. *Worlebury: An Ancient Stronghold in the County of Somerset.*

Evans, J. 1980. *Worlebury: The Story of the Iron Age Hill-Fort at Weston-super-Mare.*

Evans, J. 1980. 'Mr Pigot's Cottage near the Bristol Channel, Somerset', *Avon Past 3.*

Farr, G. 1967. *West Country Passenger Steamers.*

Granville, A.B. 1841. *Spas of England and Principal Sea-Bathing Places.*

Gough, J.W. 1967. *The Mines of Mendip.*

Hall, W.G. (ed.) 1971. *Man and the Mendips.*

Hogg, I.V. 1974. *Coast Defences of England and Wales, 1856–1956.*

Hudson, K. 1971. *The Fashionable Stone.*

Hutson, A.F. 1972. *The Development of Elementary Education in Weston-super-Mare prior to 1914* (typescript in Woodspring Central Library).

Jackson, W. 1877. *Visitors' Handbook to Weston-super-Mare.*

Knight, F.A. 1902. *The Sea-Board of Mendip.*

Maggs, C. 1964. *The Weston, Clevedon and Portishead Railway.*

Maggs, C. 1974. *The Weston-super-Mare Tramways.*

Mais, S.P.B. 1938. *Walking in Somerset.*

Palmer, W.R. 1924. *A Century of Weston-super-Mare History.*

Pawle, G. 1956. *The Secret War.*

Pevsner, N. 1958. *The Buildings of England: North Somerset and Bristol.*

Pimlott, J.A.R. 1947. *The Englishman's Holiday: a Social History.*

Plomer, W. (ed.) 1977. *Kilvert's Diary 1870–1879.*

Rutter, J. 1829. *Delineations of the North-Western Division of the County of Somerset.*

Somerset County Council 1971. *The History of Quarrying in Somerset.*

Thomas, D. St. J. 1967. *A Regional History of the Railways of Great Britain, vol. 1: The West Country.*

Tomalin, D.J. 1974. *Woodspring Priory.*

Watts, M. 1975. *Somerset Windmills.*

Wickham, A.R. 1952. *Churches of Somerset.*

Williams, M. 1970. *The Draining of the Somerset Levels.*

Williams-Ellis, C. 1947. *Weston-super-Mare: Post-War Development* (typescript in Woodspring Central Library).

The bandstand in Grove Park, erected in the 1890s once the park had been opened to the public.

Selective Index

180